Becoming a Better Lover

Becoming a Better Lover

❖

The Complete Guide to Life and Marriage

Cyndi O'Bannon

iUniverse, Inc.
New York Lincoln Shanghai

Becoming a Better Lover
The Complete Guide to Life and Marriage

iUniverse books may be ordered through booksellers or by contacting:

iUniverse
2021 Pine Lake Road, Suite 100
Lincoln, NE 68512
www.iuniverse.com
1-800-Authors (1-800-288-4677)

ISBN: 0-595-33867-4

Printed in the United States of America

1 Corinthians 13:1-8
(Good News)

I may be able to speak the languages
of human beings and even of angels,
but if I have no love,
my speech is no more
than a noisy gong or a clanging bell.

I may have the gift of inspired preaching;
I may have all knowledge and understand all secrets;
I may have all the faith needed to move mountains—
but if I have no love, I am nothing.

I may give away everything I have,
and even give up my body to be burned,
but if I have no love, this does me no good.

Love is patient and kind;
it is not jealous or conceited or proud;
love is not ill-mannered or selfish or irritable.

Love does not keep a record of wrongs;
love is not happy with evil,
but is happy with the truth.

Love never gives up;
and its faith, hope, and patience never fail.
Love is eternal.

Contents

Foreword

Never in my ministry have I seen so many marriages in crisis. Every week I hear of another family in my community breaking apart. Why? I believe it is because few couples are equipped to handle the stresses that life brings to every family. Yet there is hope! God has provided practical help in His Word.

Last year I sought to bring those answers out in a sermon series I entitled "Becoming a Better Lover." It helped to plant seeds of hope in many marriages. And nearly a year later we were fortunate to see many of those seeds sprout as more than two hundred couples rededicated their marriage vows in a church service. It was awesome!

But the ideal would be to equip couples to handle life stresses before the problems start. To answer that need, God raised up Cyndi O'Bannon. Cyndi has taken my work and done wonders with it. She has reworked it to create a dynamic premarital class that she co-teaches with her husband, Steve. And from the laboratory of those classes, this book that you hold in your hands has risen. It is tried and tested. And if you put it into action, you will see that it is true.

I am a firm believer in marriage. It is a wonderful gift from God. It is my prayer that as you read this book, whether as a group study, or just as a couple, you will experience all that God has for you through the wonderful blessing of marriage.

Pastor George Feiser
Grace Community Church
November, 2004

Preface

In January 2003, George Feiser (pastor of Grace Community Church in Plano, Texas) began an eight-week sermon series with the intriguing title "Becoming a Better Lover." Based on the thirteenth chapter of 1 Corinthians, his sermons sought to articulate the nuts and bolts of what real love looks like: how it thinks, how it acts, and what motivates it.

Midway through the series, I began to entertain thoughts that these sermons offered very practical instruction for starry-eyed lovers approaching their wedding day. Suspecting that those thoughts were prompted by the Holy Spirit, I mentioned the matter to my husband, Steve. His enthusiasm encouraged me that perhaps we had found our ministry at Grace: that of leading a marriage preparation class for engaged couples.

Pastor George greeted our idea with enthusiasm and referred us to his staff. When we approached Bob Rudy (former Care Pastor for Grace), we envisioned playing tapes of the sermons and leading a discussion afterwards. Bob encouraged us to write our own curriculum instead, adapting the sermon series specifically to the needs of engaged couples and supplementing with instruction about marriage itself. He concluded our interview by saying, "I have been praying for a couple to lead this ministry for six months."

Having had our ministry confirmed, Steve and I began to wait for God's timing in fulfilling our vision. It came in August 2003, when I lost my part-time job due to the implosion of the telecommunications industry in North Texas.

Over the last fifteen months I have written and rewritten the curriculum. My method has been straightforward. First I transcribed the sermons; then I began to study the scriptures that were quoted therein. When ideas and outlines and scriptures came to me (most frequently in the shower), I wrote them down. As key concepts began to emerge, I used a concordance to look up all the relevant scriptures. In a few instances, I went to *Strong's Exhaustive Concordance* to try to tease some clarity from the original languages.

I have always had a preference for letting the scriptures speak for themselves, and that is what I tried to do in this book. My understanding of the scriptures has been shaped by my thirty-one years of walking with the Lord Jesus and by my twenty-three years of marriage to Steve. What I have written is not abstract or theoretical; it is intensely practical to daily life, and many of the insights have been hard won.

Because of my conviction that the Bible is an intensely practical guide, I have enjoyed surveying current research in the social sciences. I have cited many of those research findings as a way of illustrating God's wisdom. Each scientific discovery about the way our bodies are created or the way we function socially seems to confirm the wisdom of the Biblical guidelines written so long ago. You see, it all fits together because it is all God's design.

It is my deep and abiding conviction that marriage is in crisis today because we have become Biblically illiterate. Without knowledge of the scriptures, we have undertaken all sorts of social "reforms" that are contrary to the way God created human beings to function. The inevitable result is heartbreak and broken lives.

> My people are *destroyed* for lack of *knowledge*…Since you have forgotten the law of your God, I also will forget your children. Hosea 4:6 (NAS)

Knowledge is needed on two levels. We need to know how God designed us to live our lives (in general), and we need to know how God designed marriage (in particular). That is why this book does not follow the customary marriage preparation format, but devotes considerable time and resources to topics such as generosity, unselfishness, forgiveness, anger, conflict, and confrontation. These are the nuts and bolts of daily life—whether inside or outside of marriage.

The institution of marriage is woefully misunderstood by popular culture today. Marriage has been reduced to a vehicle for meeting the emotional needs of its partners. Marriage is so much more, and its strength and glory come from working together to meet the needs of others. You see, emotional fulfillment is the byproduct of a healthy marriage, not the end itself. The Biblical concepts of self-denial and self-control are also woefully absent from the current mindset.

Churches have been the traditional custodians of marriage in our society. Most people still seek to be married by a minister. I believe that we can do a much better job within our churches of preparing engaged couples for marriage.

The average bride today spends six months and countless hours in planning her wedding. And yet almost no time is spent preparing for the marriage that follows. Excluding the selection of wedding gifts, she and the groom may spend a few hours in premarital counseling with the pastor who will perform their ceremony. What an imbalance!

And yet this imbalance is primarily the fault of the churches, not the engaged couples. I have found that young people are genuinely interested in the Biblical view of marriage, especially if you can help them fit the pieces together in their own minds. In fact, they often are highly motivated to make their marriages work. Having suffered the divorce (and perhaps serial monogamy) of their parents, they are determined that it will be different for their own kids.

What has been missing is a workable mechanism for the delivery of the comprehensive premarital instruction that is needed. After all, the demands on a pastor's time are already heavy. Increasingly however, churches have begun to offer classes for engaged couples led by mentoring couples. This book has been written for such a course.

The course that Steve and I teach meets two hours weekly over the course of nine weeks. The classes consist of one hour of instruction followed by one hour of discussion (the homework from the previous week). We sit around a table and have light snacks. At the end of the course, we have a ceremony where we hand out certificates and the couples make their Oneness Covenants with each other. Our course is offered three to four times yearly.

The couples that come to us reflect the culture in which they have grown up. Most are living together. Many are new to the church. It is a tremendous opportunity to reach people for Jesus, but in order to do so we must love them as Jesus did. It has been our experience that couples are unwilling to discuss their personal sin in a group environment. For that reason we added a final lesson (to be completed before they meet with the officiating pastor) so that issues of salvation and sexual sin can be addressed in a pastoral setting.

But where *sin* increased, God's *grace* increased much more. Romans 5:20 (GN)

I would like to share my enthusiasm for this ministry with others. Although weddings are frequently viewed as an inconvenience in busy church schedules, they offer unique evangelistic opportunities. There is seldom a time that individuals are more open to instruction in a Biblical worldview than when they are getting married. They have a vested interest in hearing what you say because they want their marriage to succeed. If you can be a winsome witness for Christ, then God's grace can abound in their hearts and lives.

Some of you may wonder at the hubris of the subtitle: The *Complete* Guide to Life and Marriage. Actually, the Lord and I had a similar dialog. During the final edit, I felt prompted to change the subtitle, and this was the phrase that stuck in my mind. But my essential modesty and carefulness was offended by the word "complete." I tried several other words in its place, but nothing seemed to fit. Finally, I came to understand that this book is complete in the sense that love is the Great Commandment. If you get the love part right, you will get everything else right as a matter of course.

> "*Love* the Lord your God with all your heart and with all your soul and with all your mind...*Love* your neighbor as yourself." All the Law and the Prophets *hang* on these *two* commandments. Matthew 22: 37-40 (NIV)

I close with four acknowledgements. Steve and I will always be indebted to Pastor Lester Wooten (retired pastor of Longview Christian Fellowship in Longview, Texas) and especially to his wife, Darlene, who instilled in us the understanding of marriage that we carry with us to this day.

I honor my pastor, George Feiser. His wisdom and insight are found on every page of Lessons 1-3 and Lessons 6-8, and his informal style has set the tone for this book. It has been my privilege to partner with him in making God's message accessible to our generation.

I am grateful that Steve Lucas (Teaching Pastor at Grace Community Church) has been my advisor for this project. I trust him implicitly and appreciate the confidence that he has shown in me.

Words fail in acknowledging the contributions of my husband, Steve O'Bannon—my partner in life and in ministry. His heart for God and intellectual curiosity are perfectly suited to mine. He has believed in me and encouraged me, and this book is the fruit of our lives together.

Cyndi O'Bannon
November 2004

Lesson #1: The Nature of Love

Love Is More than Feelings

Most people decide to get married because they are "in love." But being "in love" and loving are two very different things. In fact, you can be "in love" without having any real love for one another at all. None. Nada.

When Boy catches the eye of Girl and sparks fly, what you are experiencing is a hormonally based attraction which results in a rush of emotion. It's a wonderful feeling and one to be savored, but it's not real love.

"Love at first sight" means there is an initial emotional and sexual attraction between two people. What you are experiencing is infatuation. It can go on for quite a long time as you learn about each other, and it's the stuff that poets write about and movie makers film in soft focus. It's great. But one day the feelings will stop. It is inevitable.

> You looked at me, and I fell in love. One *look* my way and I was *hopelessly* in love! Song of Solomon 4:9 (Mes)

Another thing people confuse with love is lust. Infatuation and lust start with the same hormonal attraction and rush of emotion, but whereas infatuation celebrates the other person and the relationship, lust completely surrenders to sexual desire. Whereas infatuation is content to experience sexual tension as a future hope, lust insists that sexual tension be fulfilled, the sooner the better.

Lust isn't just sexual desire. After all, God created sexual desire and gave it as a good gift to his children. But he also created sexual desire for a specific purpose, the purpose of marriage. The tragedy of lust is that it severs sexual desire from its created purpose of marriage—with unintended consequences.

> Each of you should learn to *control* his own body in a way that is holy and honorable, not in passionate *lust* like the heathen, who do not know God. 1 Thessalonians 4:4-5 (NIV)

1

How can you distinguish love from lust? First of all, love focuses on the beloved, but lust focuses on itself. Moreover, love seeks to meet the needs of others, but lust demands that its own needs be met. Love is willing to wait until marriage for sexual intimacy, but lust isn't. Love exercises self-control, but lust celebrates self-indulgence. Love sets you free to be your best, but lust enslaves you to desire. Love makes you happy, but lust keeps you frustrated.

> Now *flee* from youthful *lusts* and pursue righteousness, faith, love and peace. 2 Timothy 2:22 (NAS)

Now if love is more than feelings and sexual attraction, then what in the world is it? What IS this thing called love?

➤ Love is commanded, not optional

The religious leaders of his day asked Jesus to identify the single most important rule in the entire Bible. Jesus quoted a verse from Deuteronomy. The most important thing for you to do if you want to please God is to love him, really love him with every part of your being.

> '*Love* the Lord your *God* with all your heart, with all your soul, and with all your mind.' This is the greatest and the most important commandment. Matthew 22:37-38 (GN)

Moreover, Jesus tied a second rule to the first. He quoted a verse from Leviticus. You see, love that focuses *only* on God to the exclusion of others isn't real love. The true measure of your love for God is in your love for other people.

> The second most important commandment is like it: '*Love* your *neighbor* as you love yourself.' Matthew 22:39 (GN)

In his final hours with his disciples before his arrest, Jesus sought to emphasize the importance of this second commandment. In John's gospel account, Jesus commands the disciples to love each other three separate times.

> My *command* is this: *love* each other as I have loved you. John 15:12 (NIV)

Love is very important to God; in fact, it is THE most important thing to him. You see, when you love God and you love others, your actions will fulfill every other commandment. Moreover, you will have the right attitude and the right motive in what you do.

> The *entire law* is summed up in a single command: "Love your neighbor as yourself." Galatians 5:14 (NIV)

Isn't it interesting that all this talk about love is framed as something God commands you to do? It is not optional; it is not voluntary; it is not something you can do if you feel like it. It is what God *requires* of you in any and every situation.

Now if God commands you to love others, love has to be something you can control. Love cannot be a feeling, because feelings are involuntary emotional responses; you cannot control your feelings. You can control how you express your feelings, whether you choose to act on them or not, but you cannot control your feelings themselves. And so because God commands you to love others, we know that love is not a feeling. It is not an emotion.

Please don't misunderstand. Most of the time, loving feelings will accompany real love. God has designed it this way, to help bind us closer together. But love doesn't depend on having certain feelings. Real love is something separate from your feelings; it is something you can control.

➤ Love is behavior, not feelings

Love is demonstrated by the words you say and the actions you take, not by your feelings or emotions. Your love is measured by your deeds.

> And let us consider how we may spur one another on toward *love* and good *deeds*. Hebrews 10:24 (NIV)

If your words and your deeds aren't loving, you have failed to love. It's not enough to talk a good game or to have good intentions. You have to follow through with your behavior.

> Let us stop just *saying* we love each other; let us really show it by our *actions*. 1 John 3:18 (NLT)

Now, behavior is always the result of the choices you make. Your actions and your words don't just happen to you; they are acts of your free will. You are the one who chooses to say the things you say and to do the things you do.

In the same way, love is a choice you make. In every situation, you choose your behavior: whether it will be loving or unloving, whether it will build others up or tear them down. Choosing to love (or not to love) is always an act of your will.

> I pray that your love will keep on *growing* and that you will fully know and understand how to make the right *choices*. Philippians 1:9-10 (CEV)

Some people like to talk about love as if they have no control over it. They say, "I just fell in love, I couldn't help it," as if it were like falling into a ditch. They find it convenient to equate love with *feelings* because then they don't have to take responsibility for their behavior. These same people try to justify divorce by saying, "I don't know, I just fell out of love," as if they had no control over their behavior toward their spouse. You see, they don't want to admit to themselves or others that when their feelings went away, they chose not to love their spouse.

It's easy to love when you have loving feelings. But feelings of love come and go, they ebb and flow like waves in the ocean—just as all feelings do. And when your feelings of love aren't there, when your love for your spouse is at low tide, you have a choice to make. Will you continue to act in love?

Acting in love when you don't feel like it is the greatest form of love. The real test of your love comes when things aren't going the right way, when you've lost your job and you don't have any money, when you're wondering how ends are going to meet and you're at each other's throats, when the kids are going off into left field. Real love for your spouse chooses to love him/her *regardless* of the circumstances and regardless of how you feel.

Love is like the Energizer Bunny; it just keeps going and going and going and going. Love doesn't quit when the going gets tough.

> Love *never gives up*, never loses faith, is always hopeful, and endures through every circumstance. 1 Corinthians 13:7 (NLT)

In difficult circumstances, self-control is the necessary ally of love. When the choice isn't easy, when the circumstances are bleak, or when your beloved is acting poorly, your self-control enables you to *continue* to choose to love. Self-control helps you take the long view, to believe that things will get better, and that your loving feelings will return in due season.

> For the Spirit that God has given us does not make us timid; instead, his Spirit fills us with power, *love*, and *self-control*. 2 Timothy 1:7 (GN)

Acting in love is a choice you make, either reluctantly or enthusiastically. You can be half-hearted in your efforts, or you can aggressively reach out to others with loving words and deeds. The Bible encourages you to take the initiative and actively seek out opportunities to grow in love.

> *Go after* a life of love as if your life depended on it—because it does. 1 Corinthians 14:1 (Mes)

➤ Choosing to love releases God's power

Choosing to love God is an act of your will, a step of faith. As a result, you will see God's supernatural power at work in your life, transforming you from the inside out. Each time you choose to reach out to God in love, your faith and your confidence in him will grow.

Nothing is more exciting that realizing that the God of the Universe knows your name and the details of your life. When you love God, you have a personal, intimate relationship with him.

> But the person who loves God is *known* by him. 1 Corinthians 8:3 (GN)

You can't even imagine the good things God has planned for you. But God's plans for you can't become a reality in your life until you begin to love God, because it is only then that you will trust God enough to let him direct your steps and change your heart.

> No eye has seen, no ear has heard, and no mind has *imagined* what God has prepared for those who love him. 1 Corinthians 2:9 (NLT)

There are plenty of bad things in life, and you are not exempt from them. But when you love God, he is able to work through each situation, whether it is bad or good, to produce something of lasting benefit for you. God can redeem any situation when you love him and you put your trust in him.

> We know that in *everything* God works for the good of those who love him. Romans 8:28 (NCV)

When you love God, he will provide for you. You don't have to worry about your daily needs if your focus is on the Kingdom of God. You can be confident that your needs will be met as a matter of course as you follow his direction.

So I tell you, don't *worry* about everyday life…He will give you all you need from day to day if you *live for him* and make the Kingdom of God your primary concern. Matthew 6:25-33 (NLT)

➢ Choosing to love changes you

Choosing to love others is an act of your will, but it doesn't end there. Loving others has transformational power, both for them and for you. Each time you choose to reach out to others in love, you become more like God in your thinking and more effective in your relationships.

Spiritual growth occurs in community, through the dynamic of human relationships. You weren't meant to be a Lone Ranger; you need other people if you are to reach your full potential. As others share their experiences, you can learn from them and be encouraged by them. Moreover, there are certain things about God that you can understand and experience only through your interaction with others.

Then as their hearts are *joined together* in love, they will be wonderfully blessed with complete understanding. And they will truly *know* Christ. Colossians 2:2 (CEV)

The natural result of loving others is joy. God causes joy to well up inside of you, not because of your circumstances, but because you are living as God intended you to live. God created us with a deep human longing to love and to be loved, and whenever that need is met, your heart will be joyful.

I have told you this so that you will be filled with my *joy*. Yes, your joy will *overflow*! I command you to love each other in the same way that I love you. John 15:11-12 (NLT)

Your motives determine your effectiveness in what you do and say. Unless others sense that your words are spoken in love and that your actions are undertaken in love, you will not have the positive results you desire. Love makes you productive. It makes the things you do effective. It makes you useful to God and to others.

And finally you will grow to have genuine love for everyone. The more you grow like this, the more you will become *productive* and *useful* in your knowledge of our Lord Jesus Christ. 2 Peter 1:9 (NCV)

When you love others, you are focused on what you have in common with them, instead of on your differences. Your common focus, your common interests, and your common tasks build your sense of closeness and unity with those you love. But when you feel alienated from someone—when you choose not to love him/her—you invariably are focused on your differences.

> Do all these things; but most important, love each other. Love is what holds you all *together* in perfect *unity*. Colossians 3:14 (NCV)

If you are actively demonstrating your love to others, it is easier for them to overlook your shortcomings. It is easier for others to forgive your flops, fumbles and failures when they have the larger, positive context of your loving conduct in which to judge your failure. Moreover, when they are confident of your love for them, they are not as likely to interpret your words or actions negatively when they are unsure of your motive or meaning.

> Most important of all, continue to show deep love for each other, for love *covers* a multitude of *sins*. 1 Peter 4:8 (NLT)

Love is a wonderful motivating force. You see, love motivates us and energizes us. When you are motivated by love, you are able to do things joyously that would otherwise be tedious, tiresome, or overwhelming.

> For we remember before our God and Father how you put your faith into practice, how your love made you *work so hard*, and how your hope in our Lord Jesus Christ is firm. 1 Thessalonians 1:3 (GN)

God Evaluates You by Your Relationships

Of everything that you do in your life, loving God and loving others are the most important things to God. Nothing that you do is more important. Nothing matters more to God.

> The *commandment* that God has given us is: "Love God and love each other!" 1 John 4:21 (CEV)

Love is the very essence of God's nature, and it is the very essence of his relationship with you. God created you to love you! And when your disobedience and your rebellion separated you from God, he sent Jesus to defeat the power of sin through his sacrifice on the cross.

> This is love: not that we loved God, but that *he loved us* and sent his Son as an atoning sacrifice for our sin**s**. 1 John 4:10 (NIV)

Experiencing God's love transforms you. His love fills your heart to overflowing, spilling out to those around you. The natural result of being loved by God is loving others. It is impossible to have a relationship with God without having love in your heart for others.

> God is love, and anyone who doesn't love others *has never known* him. 1 John 4:8 (CEV)

Love is not an abstraction to God; nor is it warm and fuzzy feelings. Unless love manifests itself in tangible behavior to the *people* in your world, it is not real love.

> But if we say we love God and don't *love each other*, we are liars. We cannot see God. So how can we love God, if we don't love the people we can see? 1 John 4:20 (CEV)

Your relationships matter to God. In fact, your relationships are the principal way that God perfects his love in you. Most of your spiritual growth will come as you seek to love each other through the flops, fumbles, and failures of life. Moreover, your love for your spouse can bring God's healing and ministry into his/her life.

> No one has ever seen God, but if we love each other, God lives in us, and his love is *made perfect* in us. 1 John 4:12 (NCV)

One day you will give an account to God. He will judge your works on earth in order to determine your responsibilities in heaven. And the primary thing he will want to know about is your relationships, especially your relationship with your spouse and your kids.

> ➢ **Love makes your words effective**

Nothing you say matters without love. No matter how well spoken you are, no matter how true your words are, no matter how eloquent or engaging you are when you speak them, your words will be ineffective unless they are spoken with love. Without love, your words are just noise.

> If I could speak in any language in heaven or on earth but didn't love others, I would only be making *meaningless noise* like a loud gong or a clanging cymbal. 1 Corinthians 13:1 (NLT)

You see, it is your relationship with a person that makes your words effective, not the words themselves. When others feel loved and respected by you, they will listen to what you say. But if they don't sense your love, they will tune you out.

Moreover, your love for others will shape your message. It will temper your words, making them less strident and less accusatory. You will tailor your message to your listeners, making it more accessible to them and presenting it from their point of view.

Similarly, nothing you know matters without love. It doesn't matter how smart you are or how much you know. You see, it is not how much you *know* but how much you *care* that determines whether your knowledge is of any benefit to others. No matter how much you know, your listeners will tune you out if they don't feel loved and respected by you.

> If I had the gift of prophecy, and if I *knew all* the mysteries of the future and knew everything about everything, but didn't love others, *what good* would I be? 1 Corinthians 13:2 (NLT)

Unless you are motivated by love, your knowledge will make you arrogant. You will be impressed with yourself and focused on demonstrating your intellectual superiority. You will have no interest in shaping your message and using your knowledge to benefit others.

> Knowledge *puffs* up, but love builds up. 1 Corinthians 8:1 (NIV)

➤ **Love makes your actions productive**

Nothing you do matters without love. Your accomplishments do not make you useful or give you significance. Your love is what makes you useful and gives your life significance.

> And if I had the gift of *faith* so that I could speak to a mountain and make it move, without love I would be *no good* to anybody. 1 Corinthians 13:2 (NLT)

It doesn't matter how great your accomplishment is. In the spiritual realm, you could work miracles. In the business world, you could build a Fortune 500 company. In the scientific world, you could win a Nobel Prize. In the athletic world, you could set a new world record. In the religious world, you could build a superchurch. In the legal world, you could argue a case before the Supreme Court. You could even be Man of the Year for *TIME Magazine*.

Your usefulness lies not in what you achieve, but in the lives you touch along the way. If you don't touch people's lives with God's love, what good are your accomplishments?

In addition, love will make anything you undertake more *productive*. No matter how smart your plan, how well it is executed, how good your intentions, or how much the change is needed, your actions will not produce the desired result if they are done without love. Your love is what causes your actions to be well-received and your motives to be trusted. This is true in the business world and the political realm no less than at home or church. As Jesus said, loving others enables you to bear much fruit.

> If a man remains in me and I in him, he will *bear much fruit*…My command is this: Love each other as I have loved you. John 15:5-12 (NIV)

Similarly, nothing you give matters without love. It doesn't matter how large your gift is, how big a personal sacrifice you make, or how greatly the gift is needed. Unless you give it in love, your gift doesn't produce the intended benefit—for yourself or for others.

> If I *give everything* I own to the poor and even go to the stake to be burned as a martyr, but I don't love, I've *gotten nowhere*. 1 Corinthians 13:3 (Mes)

Giving is not always a sign of love and selflessness. In fact, many people give for very selfish reasons, without any love or concern for others at all. This happens when they give you something in order to obligate you to *give* something back to them.

Other people give in order to control the behavior of those they give to, in order to obligate them to *do* certain things in return. A lot of parents bargain with their kids in this way. Some parents keep their adult kids connected to them by controlling the purse strings. This type of giving is very manipulative and dishonest, and it has nothing to do with real love.

Some people give to others in order to feel better about themselves. They need the prestige and recognition that come from making a sizeable gift. What motivates them is the plaque on the wall, the picture in the newspaper, the special reception for donors, the name on the building.

> When you give to the poor, don't be like the hypocrites. They *blow trumpets* in the synagogues and on the streets so that people will see them and *honor* them. I tell you the truth, those hypocrites already have their full reward. Matthew 6:2 (NCV)

Still others people give in order to appease their guilty consciences. Many parents try to compensate for their lack of time with their kids by buying them things. This type of giving does nothing to meet the real needs of others, and it is powerless to help you grow in authentic love.

➤ Relationships mean more than accomplishments

Most of the time our lives are focused on activities: going to work, going to school, going to the store, cooking a meal, cleaning the house, working out, mowing the lawn, servicing the car, going to church, going to the movies. In fact, activities are probably the only things you list on your calendar.

But if you were to take the sum of your life, most of these activities wouldn't even rate a footnote. Your relationships and your character are what would matter most, not just to God but to you as well. You can see this in funeral eulogies, when the legacy of your life is measured in the lives you touched and the character you showed in your relationships.[1] In the same vein, retirement send-offs are long on anecdotes that reveal your character and short on the details of your successful business deals.

Furthermore, what is it that matters most to those who are closest to you? It's a safe bet your child cares much more about whether you are around at night than whether you get that promotion to the next level.[2] It's much more important to your toddler that you play games with him/her than that you get an advanced degree. Your spouse would probably prefer to be loved by you than to have every material thing that his/her heart desired. Your teenager needs you around to monitor his/her schoolwork, activities, and friends much more that he/she needs a fat allowance or new car.

During the September 11th tragedy, people didn't call their customers to finish a business deal or their brokers to place a final trade. They called their husbands, wives, fathers, and mothers to express their love and to say good-bye.

When they had to choose the most important thing in their lives, they chose their relationships, not their resumes.

Without relationships, everything you accomplish is meaningless. Wealth, status, and professional achievements mean little if there is no one to share them with.

> What do people get for all their hard work?...Everything under the sun is meaningless, like *chasing the wind*. Ecclesiastes 1:3-14 (NLT)

It is possible to be so focused on your accomplishments, financial success, career advancement, status, and recognition, that you miss the truly important things in life. Many people meet the goals they have set for themselves only to discover that satisfaction and fulfillment continue to elude them. You see, God has created you so that lasting fulfillment comes only through your relationships—with God and with others.

> What good is it for a man to gain the whole *world*, yet forfeit his *soul?* Mark 8:36 (NIV)

For this reason, it is absolutely essential that you give your relationships priority in your life. As a Christian, God should be your first priority, because his hand sustains and directs you. As a husband or wife, your spouse should be your second priority, behind only God. When you have children, your family should be your third priority.

These three relationships all take priority over your work. Please don't misunderstand. Your work is very important: as a means of providing for your family, for your personal integrity, and as a witness to others. Moreover, your work will necessarily consume the largest chunk of your day. Ranking work as your fourth priority doesn't diminish its importance; it only serves to emphasize how important your relationships with God, your spouse, and your children truly are.

Making your relationships a priority requires you to invest in them. You can't take them for granted. You must nurture them frequently. You need to invest yourself emotionally in meeting the needs of your spouse and children. Just going through the motions isn't enough. You must be devoted to them.

> Be *devoted* to one another in brotherly love; give preference to one another in honor. Romans 12:10 (NAS)

Keep Growing In Love

Love isn't static. It isn't something you either have or don't have. Love is something that grows, just like your faith grows. Moreover, spiritual growth is the kind of thing that doesn't stand still. Either you are gaining ground and growing in love, or you are losing ground and becoming more selfish.

> We always have good reason to thank God for you, because your faith in God and your love for each other *keep growing* all the time. 2 Thessalonians 1:3 (CEV)

What can you do to grow in love? How can you build real love into your life? Here are some suggestions to help you get started.

➢ Learn from Christ's example

God has given us an example of real love in Jesus. His life among us was a demonstration of authentic, powerful, selfless love.

> Live a life filled with love for others, following the *example of Christ*, who loved you and gave himself as a sacrifice to take away your sins. Ephesians 5:2 (NLT)

The best way to learn about love is to experience the love that God has for you. You see, the way God loves you is the way you should love others. The way God deals with you in difficult or disappointing situations is the way that you should deal with others.

> Observe *how Christ loved us*. His love was not cautious but extravagant. He didn't love in order to get something from us but to give everything of himself to us. Love like that. Ephesians 5:2 (Mes)

Little children learn by imitating others. They imitate the behavior of others, the words they use, and the attitudes they show. At first, children simply imitate the behavior without understanding it. But over time, they come to understand the motives behind the behavior, and they experience the emotions that come from the behavior. We learn love in the same way. We begin by choosing to act in a loving way, and in doing so we grow in love.

> Be *imitators* of God, therefore, as dearly loved children. Ephesians 5:1 (NIV)

➤ Rely on Christ's love within you

Human love runs out. Sometimes you are in a tunnel of testing and chaos, and you can't think straight or remember why you loved your beloved in the first place. Sometimes you are simply exhausted, having given until you don't have anything left to give. Sometimes other people annoy or alienate you, and you can't bring yourself to be nice to them, much less love them.

You see, human love eventually runs out. Fortunately God's love never runs out. God always has an inexhaustible supply of love for you.

> And so we know and *rely on* the love God has for us. 1 John 4:16 (NIV)

When you rely on God, you experience the love God has for you. And as God pours his love into your heart, it overflows out to others. By relying on God's love, you can have an inexhaustible supply of love for others.

> God has *poured* out his *love* into our hearts by the Holy Spirit, whom he has given us. Romans 5:5 (NIV)

The first step you must take in order to grow in love is to establish a relationship with the God who can give you that kind of love. If you have not already done so, you need to invite God into your heart, allowing him to clean house and to set up residence there. Only then can you experience God's love.

> I ask him to strengthen you by his Spirit—not a brute strength but a glorious inner strength—that Christ will live in you as you *open* the door and *invite* him in. Ephesians 3:16-17 (Mes)

Now, having a relationship with God is not a one-time event. No relationship is. For example, marriage is much more than a wedding ceremony. In fact, your wedding is just the *beginning* of your married life, not its completion. It is no different with God.

Once you establish a relationship with God, you need to sustain it. Each day you must open your heart to Jesus, invite him to take control of your life, trust him to meet your needs, and receive the love he has for you. You have begun a lifetime journey with God, and you cannot yet conceive just how much he loves you.

> May you experience the love of Christ, though it is so *great* you will never fully *understand* it. Then you will be filled with the fullness of life and power that comes from God. Ephesians 3:18-19 (NLT)

God's love is inexhaustible. It is extravagant. It is so great that you will never fully understand it. But if you want God's love for others, you must first experience the love God has for you.

Now some of you have a hard time believing that you are loveable—because that's the way you've been treated in the past. But God doesn't think you're unlovable. His love for you is extravagant and unconditional, and it will never run out. And so, if you want to grow in love, you must dare to believe that God really loves *you*.

➢ Memorize what God says about love

Personal change only comes by changing your thoughts, your attitudes, and your perspective. And the perspective you need to grow in love is found only in the Bible.

> Let the *words of Christ*, in all their richness, *live in your hearts* and make you wise...sing psalms and hymns and spiritual songs to God with thankful hearts. Colossians 3:16 (NLT)

Some of you find it easier to memorize Bible verses than others do. Singing is an excellent way to memorize scripture, because the melody and the rhythm give you something to pin the words onto. In fact, singing God's word dates to the Old Testament and has been used extensively throughout church history.

If you have difficulty memorizing whole verses perfectly, focus on the key phrases in the passage. You see, when you get into a situation where you need God's help, it will probably be a phrase that God brings to your mind. And when you are meditating on God's word, it will probably be a phrase that keeps turning over and over in your mind as you ponder what it means and how you might apply it in your life.

In this regard, you may find that the older, more poetic translations (such as the King James, the New American Standard, and the New International versions) are easier to memorize. Their sentences are often lyrical, and their words frequently provide a memorable turn of phrase.

To begin, choose a verse or two from this lesson that stand out to you. Write each one down on an index card, post it in a prominent place, or add it to the screen-saver of your computer. Incidentally, writing out the words of scripture is also an excellent way to memorize them.

➤ Start your day with a reminder to love

The first ten minutes of your day can set your mood for the whole day. And so when you get up in the morning, you need to remind yourself that you want to grow in love today.

You may do so by reading a Bible verse that you have memorized or are trying to memorize. You may do it through prayer, by simply saying, "God, I want to love you today, and I want to love others like I should." Choose something that works for you, and make it part of your daily schedule.

> In the *morning*, O Lord, you hear my voice; in the morning I lay my requests before you and wait in *expectation*. Psalm 5:3 (NIV)

You see, you need to start your day with God. And then you need to expect him to work through the opportunities of your day to help you grow in love.

➤ Practice acting in unselfish ways

> The things you have learned and received and heard and seen in me, *practice* these things. Philippians 4:9 (NAS)

Practice makes perfect, does it not? How many of you were experts the first time you got behind the wheel of a car? None of you were. You were all awkward, and you all made mistakes. Yet now driving has become second nature to you.

The same is true in this whole area of loving. You will have to do some things very consciously at first, until the behaviors become second nature to you. You see, there is no such thing as a natural born lover. Loving others is *learned* through practice.

> He…who comes to me and hears my words and puts them into *practice*…is like a man building a house, who dug down deep and laid the foundation on rock. When a flood came, the torrent struck that house but could not shake it, because it was *well built*. Luke 6:47-48 (NIV)

If you want your marriage to be strong, you have to put your love into practice. You need to practice acting in unselfish ways so that you will be ready for the torrents and the chaos of life.

➤ Fellowship with other loving people

We learn from others. We learn by listening to their words, watching what they do, and seeing how they respond in difficult situations. You can't learn to love in a vacuum; you need relationships with other loving people.

> And let us consider how we may *spur one another on* toward love and good deeds. Let us not give up meeting together, as some are in the habit of doing, but let us *encourage* one another. Hebrews 10:24-25 (NIV)

The benefit of fellowship with others goes beyond learning how to love. Being with other loving people motivates you to want to love. As you observe their behavior and as they share their stories, something will rise up in you and say, "If they can do it, I can do it, too!"

Homework
Lesson #1: The Nature of Love

Love Is More than Feelings

1. Which statement in this section was the most helpful to you? Why?

Love is a command not, a option. It helps me ground the real meaning of love. Love your god with heart soul & mind

2. Which of the scripture verses quoted in this section is your favorite? Why?

Love your neighbor as yourself. I have always treated people the way I would want to be treated.

3. What role has infatuation played in your relationship? Where are you now?

NO infatuation

Happy - Loved & in love!

4. What role has lust played in your relationship? Where are you now?

No lust

5. Think of a time when your love was a choice instead of a feeling. What happened?

God Evaluates You by Your Relationships

6. Which statement in this section was the most helpful to you? Why?

Nothing you say matters without love! I always say what I feel with conviction!

7. Which of the scripture verses quoted in this section is your favorite? Why?

God is love, and anyone who doesn't love others has never known him. Its the Basis of who we are as people!

8. When have you experienced God's love? How did it change you?

When I was young and wealth but my world was falling apart. I had the strength thru god to turn my life around on my own, Police, not drinking ect . . . .

9. When has your love for God caused you to love others? Please explain.

on my police job everyday, I see peoples Hardships daily. I always help or give good advice.

10. When have you given to others for selfish reasons? Please explain.

11. Do you know someone who tries to control you by his/her giving?

NO

Keep Growing in Love

12. Which statement in this section was the most helpful to you? Why?

Live a life filled with love for others
Follow the example of christ.
If he can do it so can I. or (we)

13. Which of the scripture verses quoted in this section is your favorite? Why?

God has poured out his love into our
hearts by the Holy spirit. whom
he has given us.
We all have the ability to love. (learn)

14. Have you ever tried to memorize Bible verses? What strategy works best for you?

Not really, I like to read it for better absorption.

15. How do you start your day? Is acknowledging God a part of your routine?

Yes, pray throughout the day.

16. When have you been encouraged by someone else's example in a difficult situation?

When I see handicap people it makes me feel blessed.

Lesson #2: Becoming a Giver

Develop a Giving Attitude

Loving people are "givers." They give freely to other people. Because they have a natural focus on the well-being of others, their behavior is full of loving words and loving actions.

In stark contrast are the "takers" of this world. It is not that they intend to be unloving or that they consciously plan to be hard or selfish. It's just that they are so focused on getting what they want and on getting their own needs met, that it never *occurs* to them to think about the needs of others. As a result, these people don't exhibit much loving behavior.

> Love does not *demand* its *own* way. 1 Corinthians 13:5 (NLT)

Now sometimes "takers" have a hard time recognizing themselves. This is because when it finally occurs to them to think about the other people in their world, they experience warm and fuzzy emotions that they think of as love. However, these emotions seldom get translated into real love—into actual behavior that chooses someone else's well-being over their own.

One of the best ways to distinguish "givers" from "takers" is in the timing of their loving behavior. "Givers" give in response to the need of the other person. In contrast, "takers" give when they feel like it or whenever they have a desire to connect with others. You see, "takers" love based upon their own needs, but "givers" love based upon the needs of others.

Real love is *aware* of others' needs. In fact, the Bible says that you will be cursed if you close your eyes to those in need. Now, some of you are naturally aware of the needs of others, but some of you will have to train yourselves to be aware of those needs. Some of you will have to work at it.

> Giving to the poor will keep you from poverty, but if you *close your eyes* to their needs, everyone will *curse* you. Proverbs 28:27 (CEV)

In addition, the Bible makes it clear that the time to respond to someone's need is *when* the person has the need—not tomorrow, not next week, not when it fits conveniently into your schedule. You see, real love doesn't procrastinate. It is willing to be inconvenienced.

> Don't tell your neighbor to come back *tomorrow*, if you can help *today*. Proverbs 3:28 (CEV)

➤ Giving begins with God

Unselfish giving is rooted in your relationship with God. You see, no one gives more generously and more unselfishly than God does.

> God gives *generously* and graciously to all. James 1:5 (GN)

In fact, a hallmark of God's giving is that he gives even to those who don't deserve it.

> For he makes his sun to shine on *bad* and good people alike, and gives rain to those who do good and to those who do *evil*. Matthew 5:45 (GN)

God's most precious gift to you is the ability to know him intimately and to have his life live in you. Your relationship with God is itself a measure of his generosity. You see, you don't deserve the very thing that makes your relationship with God possible: Jesus' sacrifice for your sins.

> But God demonstrates his own love for us in this: *While we were still sinners, Christ died for us.* Romans 5:8 (NIV)

It is your experience of receiving much more than you deserve from God (not just at salvation but on an ongoing basis in your daily life) that enables you to give freely to others. Gratitude for God's generosity fills your heart and mind to overflowing and spills out in generosity toward others.

> *Freely* you received, *freely* give. Matthew 10:8 (NAS)

Sometimes when you think of giving, you think of money and tangible objects. And it is important to give these things. However, the most important thing you have to give is yourself. Furthermore, if you are unwilling to give your-self, none of the other things you try to give as a substitute for your time and your attention will matter to others.

> And they gave in a way we did not expect: They first gave *themselves* to the Lord and to us. This is what God wants. 2 Corinthians 8:5 (NCV)

➤ Giving to others is giving to God

In the parable of the Last Judgment (found in Matthew 25:31-46), Jesus says that one of the most important ways you give to God is by giving to *others*. No matter how unimportant they may seem to you, God cares about them. In God's economy, whatever you do for others is service to God, and whatever you give to others is given to God.

> Then the ones who pleased the Lord will ask, "*When* did we give you some-thing to eat or drink? *When* did we welcome you as a stranger or give you clothes to wear or visit you while you were sick or in jail?" The king will answer, "Whenever you did it for any of my *people*, no matter how unimpor-tant they seemed, you did it for me." Matthew 25:37-40 (CEV)

God wants to touch others with his love through you. You can be God's instrument in a difficult situation. Your hands can be God's hands, and your ears can be God's ears for someone in need.

> Never walk away from someone who deserves help; your *hand* is God's *hand* for that person. Proverbs 3:27 (Mes)

Now sometimes people hesitate to respond to the needs of others because they feel inadequate. They think they don't have *enough* to give. But that is missing the point. It is not what you have to give that makes the difference; it's whether you give what you have.

> Here is a boy with *five small* barley loaves and *two small* fish, but how far will they go among *so many*? John 6:9 (NIV)

When Jesus fed the Five Thousand, he used the boy's lunch of five rolls and two fish as a tangible starting point. The miracle of multiplication, of enough food for five thousand men plus women and children, came *after* the young man gave his lunch to Jesus. So it is with you. When you give what you have to others, God is able to use your gift in ways you might never have imagined.

> Jesus then took the loaves, *gave thanks*, and *distributed* to those who were seated as much as they wanted. He did the same with the fish. John 6:11 (NIV)

In fact, what you have to give can sometimes be better than what others think they need. The beggar at the Temple Gate was focused on getting money for food, but Peter recognized that his greatest need wasn't money, but the ability to work for his own food. And so instead of money, which he didn't have, Peter gave the beggar something much better. He healed him!

> But Peter said, "I don't have any money for you. But *I'll give you what I have.* In the name of Jesus Christ of Nazareth, get up and walk!" Acts 3:6 (NLT)

> ➢ **Give generously**

God loves the "givers" of this world, but he despises those who only take from others.

> The *wicked* borrow and do not repay, but the *righteous* give generously. Psalm 37:21 (NIV)

Moreover, the type of giving that pleases God is generosity. God wants you to give freely with an "open" hand, not one that tries to take something back. He wants you to give more than you have to out of a thankful heart that seeks to bless others as you yourself have been blessed.

Generosity always produces more generosity. When you are generous to others, they tend to be generous in return. But more importantly, your generosity to others enables God to show greater generosity toward you.

> A generous man will prosper; he who *refreshes* others will himself be *refreshed*. Proverbs 11:25 (NIV)

This is a principle you can see in the natural world. When a farmer is stingy in planting, sowing only a few seeds, he doesn't get much of a harvest. But when he is generous in planting, sowing a great many seeds, he gets a large and generous harvest. You see, the farmer cannot *reap* what he did not *sow*. And neither can you.

> Remember this—a farmer who plants only a few seeds will get a *small* crop. But the one who plants generously will get a *generous* crop. 2 Corinthians 9:6 (NLT)

Stinginess is a stupid strategy for your life. Instead of ending up with more of the things that are valuable to you, you end up with less. You see, taking from others without giving anything back does not bring *increase* to your life. It just runs others off. In contrast, when you are generous to others, you experience much increase in your life—both from others and from God.

> It is possible to give *freely* and become more wealthy, but those who are *stingy* will lose everything. Proverbs 11:24 (NLT)

Nowhere is this more true than in relationships. And so, if you want increase in your life—if you want better, more intimate relationships with others—then you need to be sure that you give generously to others.

Jesus used a word picture to describe generosity. He called it giving a *good measure*. It's the picture of a merchant measuring out a quantity of grain, shaking the container as he fills it in order to get more grain in, continuing to fill the container until the top is mounded and begins to spill over. It's the same idea as the Baker's Dozen, of adding an extra item for good measure.

> Give and it will be given to you. They will pour into your lap a *good measure*—pressed down, shaken together, and running over. For by your standard of measure it will be *measured* to you in return. Luke 6:38 (NAS)

That's the kind of measure God wants you to give. Because what you receive from God and others will be measured with—and limited by—the measure that you use when you give to others.

➢ Don't expect anything in return

The "takers" of this world give in order to get something back. But that's not really giving is it? It's manipulation, and it has nothing to do with genuine love.

But the "givers" of this world give out of genuine love. They don't expect anything in return; they aren't concerned with how others might be useful to them in the future. They simply respond with love to the needs of others.

> But love your enemies, and do good, and lend, *expecting nothing* in return; and your reward will be great, and you will be *sons* of the Most High; for He Himself is kind to ungrateful and evil men. Luke 6:35 (NAS)

The best motivation for giving to others is your gratitude to God for his goodness to you. God gives freely to you even though you can never repay him. Moreover, he provides you what you need—not what you deserve—because he loves you. Out of gratitude, shouldn't you show the same love to others?

> But when you give a reception, invite the *poor*, the crippled, the lame, the blind, and you will be blessed, since they do not have the means to *repay* you; for you will be *repaid* at the resurrection of the righteous. Luke 14:13-14 (NAS)

Jesus wants you to give to those who cannot repay you because he understands that those who give are happier than those who receive. You see, the act of giving changes your heart, your mind, and your will. When you give to someone who cannot repay you, you *empty* yourself of some of your selfishness, and as a result, there is more room for God in your life. What a trade-off! Less selfishness and more God! No wonder you are happier.

> I have shown you in all things that by working hard in this way we must help the weak, remembering the words that the Lord Jesus himself said, "There is more *happiness* in *giving* than in receiving." Acts 20:35 (GN)

However, when you give reluctantly, when you give only because you feel forced to do so, you miss out on the blessing that giving brings. When this happens, you need to ask God for direction. It may be that you are struggling with selfishness, and what you need to do is empty yourself of selfishness before you give your gift. Or it could be that you are seeking to give the *wrong* thing, something that God has not called you to give, and that is the reason why you have not experienced joy in your giving. Whatever the reason, you should always wait to give until you can give freely and joyfully.

Each one must do just as he has purposed in his heart, not *grudgingly* or under compulsion, for God loves a *cheerful* giver. 2 Corinthians 9:7 (NAS)

Be a Good Listener

One of the best ways to give to others is simply to listen to them. In fact, "givers" are almost always good listeners because they are concerned about the needs of others. In contrast, "takers" are typically very poor listeners because they are pre-occupied with themselves and what is going on in their own world.

➤ Listen more than you talk

Many of you like talking about yourselves and your problems much more than you like listening to others talk about themselves and their problems. Some of you may actually be motormouths! In the same way that nature abhors a vac-uum, you are uncomfortable with silence and rush to fill it up with your words. In fact, you may be so busy talking that it doesn't even occur to you to give others a chance to get a word in edgewise.

But the Bible says you need to listen more than you talk. You need to train yourself to stop talking. You need to learn to make room for others to talk about the things that matter to them.

My dear brothers and sisters, always be *willing* to listen and *slow* to speak. James 1:19 (NCV)

Others of you are the "strong, silent types" who don't like anyone to do much talking. While some of you are very comfortable with silence, others of you thrive on loud music, constant TV, and video games. Either way, you find talking about feelings, hopes, and problems unsettling and pointless. And you find listening to others talk about such things boring and a waste of time.

But the Bible says you need to be willing to listen to them. You need to train yourself to pay attention when others are talking. You need to care enough about them to be willing to listen to the things that matter to them.

One of the benefits of listening to others is that you can learn things you don't know. In fact, when you listen to and learn from others, you can often save your-self from the embarrassment of saying something stupid.

The *wise* person listens to *learn* more. Proverbs 18:15 (NCV)

In addition, listening helps you get to know others better. By listening to others you learn their likes and dislikes, their problems and their successes, what is important to them and what isn't. When you learn their personal history, you gain context for their present problems. When you learn their hopes and dreams, you can better understand the emotional meaning certain events have for them.

Listen to what I say and try to *understand.* Matthew 15:10 (NLT)

Now in order to be a good listener, you need to develop an ear for when people want to talk and when they need to be listened to. You need to be attentive to the cries for help that others give. If you are not aware of others, if you are caught up in your own little world, you will miss their cry—and the opportunity—entirely.

Hear my prayer, O Lord; let my *cry* for help come to you. Psalm 102:1 (NIV)

➤ Listen for the heart message

Not all cries for help are verbal ones. Sometimes, people don't feel free to say what they are thinking and feeling. At other times, they don't have the self-awareness to put what is bothering them into words. Generally, the more painful a situation, the less able others are to put their thoughts and feelings into words, and the more likely they are to use nonverbal cues to express themselves.

Frequently during an argument one spouse will say to another, "Well, if that's the way you feel you should have said so!" But the truth is, your spouse probably didn't have the awareness to say so until the words came tumbling out of his/her mouth. You see, sometimes your words are the very last things to express what is really bothering you.

That is why it is so helpful to develop sensitivity to your spouse's body language: the shrug of the shoulder, the refusal to make eye-contact, the dejected slump, the turn of the body away from you, the moments of silence between the sentences. These nonverbal cues will help you understand when something is wrong. They will help you be attuned to your spouse's heart message.

The Gospel of Luke records an incident when a woman communicated very clearly to Jesus even though she didn't say a single word. She didn't have to, because her actions spoke for her.

> She brought an alabaster jar of perfume, and as she stood behind (Jesus) at his feet weeping, she began to wet his feet with her *tears*. Then she wiped them with her hair, *kissed* them and poured *perfume* on them. Luke 7:37-38 (NIV)

Interestingly, Jesus was the only person who understood what she was doing because he was the only one listening to her heart message. Jesus saw in her extravagant actions the heart of one who had been set free from her sins. But Simon and the other guests saw only the externals, a woman with a sinful life.

> Therefore, I tell you, her many sins have been *forgiven*—for she loved *much*. But he who has been forgiven little loves *little*. Luke 7:47 (NIV)

➢ Listen in order to comfort others

If you want to comfort others, frequently the best thing you can do is just listen to them. Listening to others shows respect for them. It demonstrates that what they have to say is important to you. It lets them know that they matter to you. It affirms that their fears and concerns deserve to be taken seriously, that their pain is real, and that they aren't losing their minds.

> If you want to offer *comfort*, then *listen* to me. Job 21:2 (CEV)

Frequently, the most comforting thing you can say to others is to say nothing at all. Your physical presence and empathetic listening let others know that you share their sorrow.

Moreover, listening to others helps them sort out the problem for themselves. Letting others talk about their pain and confusion helps them make sense of their world. Listening to them rant about the wrong that was done to them helps them sort out their feelings. Listening to them ramble on about what they could have or should have done in response to a situation helps them develop workable solutions to the problems.

> *Share* each other's *troubles* and problems, and in this way obey the law of Christ. Galatians 6:2 (NLT)

You see, the purpose of listening is not to come up with solutions to other people's problems. The purpose of listening is to support others emotionally while they sort out the problem for themselves.

Furthermore, being listened to gives others the courage they need to face their problems. Listening to others encourages them by making them feel valued, cared for, and supported. Because you care enough to listen, others know that they are not alone. By knowing that they are not alone, they gain the courage they need to face their problems and work through them.

> You will *listen*, O Lord, to the prayers of the lowly; you will give them *courage*. Psalm 10:17 (GN)

Show Kindness to Others

> Love is...*kind*. 1 Corinthians 13:4 (NLT)

Kindness combines compassion with action. That is why kindness is so powerful. You see, your concern and tenderness for others mean little if you don't follow through with the concrete help they need.

> If you know someone who doesn't have any clothes or food, you shouldn't *just say*, "I hope all goes well for you. I hope you will be warm and have plenty to eat." What good is it to say this, unless you *do something* to help? James 2:15-16 (CEV)

But material help alone is inadequate, too. Action without compassion falls short because it does not meet the emotional and spiritual needs of the person.

> Ruth answered, "You are very kind to me, sir. You have made me feel *better* by speaking *gently* to me." Ruth 2:13 (GN)

When you show kindness to someone, you nurture yourself as well as the other person. Kindness warms your heart, brightens your day, and fills you with a sense of well-being.

> Your own soul is *nourished* when you are *kind*, but you destroy yourself when you are cruel. Proverbs 11:17 (NLT)

In the Bible, patience and kindness are often mentioned together. That is because people who need your kindness often require your patience as well. You see, many people who need your help do not respond as quickly as you would like, and they may continue to need you long after the novelty has worn off for you.

> Love is *patient* and *kind*. 1 Corinthians 13:4 (NLT)

Fortunately, kindness and patience are not something you have to manufacture yourself. They are produced by God's work in you as he changes your desires and your thoughts. Kindness and patience are the natural effect, or fruit, of the Holy Spirit's work in your life.

> But when the Holy Spirit *controls* our lives, he will produce this kind of *fruit* in us: love, joy, peace, patience, kindness, goodness, faithfulness, gentleness, and self-control. Galatians 5:22-23 (NLT)

➤ Kindness begins with compassion

Compassion is what motivates you to reach out to others and try to help them. Without compassion you would just keep going on about your own business.

In the parable of the Prodigal Son, it was the father's compassion for his son that caused him to go out to meet him, to embrace him, and to receive him as a son.

> But while he was still a long way off, his father saw him and felt *compassion* for him, and *ran and embraced* him and kissed him. Luke 15:20 (NAS)

It was Jesus' compassion for the sick and disabled among the crowds that came to see him that caused him to stop what he was doing and heal them.

> When Jesus landed and saw a large crowd, he had *compassion* on them and *healed* their sick. Matthew 14:14 (NIV)

It was Jesus' compassion for the hunger of the crowd who had come to hear him that caused him to feed the Four Thousand before he sent them home.

> I have *compassion* for these people; they have already been with me three days and have nothing to eat. I do not want to send them away *hungry*. Matthew 15:32 (NIV)

It was Jesus' compassion for the ignorance of the people who had come to meet him on the shore that caused him to stop there and teach them.

> A vast crowd was there as he stepped from the boat, and he had *compassion* on them because they were like sheep without a shepherd. So he *taught* them many things. Mark 6:34 (NLT)

Now compassion (or empathy) has two components. The **cognitive component** is the ability to put yourself in someone else's situation and to see the situation from the other person's point of view.[1]

In the parable of the Good Samaritan, the Samaritan man had compassion on the Jewish robbery victim. He responded to the victim's humanity, to his pain and blood and helplessness. By focusing on what they had in common, he was able to adopt the victim's point of view.[2] Had he focused on their differences, on the longstanding animosity between Jew and Samaritan, he would never have stopped to help him.

> But a *Samaritan*, who was on a journey, came upon him; and when he saw him, he felt *compassion*, and came to him and bandaged up his *wounds*, pouring oil and wine on them. Luke 10:33-34 (NAS)

In addition, the **affective component** of empathy is the ability to feel what someone else must be feeling.[3] Because the Samaritan was able to assume the victim's point of view, he was able to connect emotionally with him. He could "feel his pain."

> *Weep* with those who *weep*. Romans 12:15 (NAS)

Some of you intuitively understand just how important it is to share the sorrow of those who are hurting. Others of you are more inclined to say things like, "Just get over it, will you?" or "That's nothing, I've experienced much worse." But compassion does not belittle the hurt of others. It acknowledges the full extent of the pain.

Nor does compassion pretend not to see the pain of others. In the parable of the Good Samaritan, the first person to reach the robbery victim was a Jewish priest. But lacking compassion for the victim, he just kept on walking, pretending not to see the man.

A *priest* happened to be going down the same road, and when he saw the man, he passed by *on the other side*. Luke 10:31 (NIV)

God doesn't ignore your cry when you are hurt or in trouble. And you shouldn't ignore the pain of others, either. You need to develop a heart full of compassion.

He does not *ignore* those who *cry* to him for help. Psalm 9:12 (NLT)

➢ Kindness is shown by your actions

It's not enough to be aware of a problem. It's not enough to have compassion for those who are hurting. You need to DO something about it. You need to take action. Love is more than feelings. Love is a choice you make concerning your behavior.

Many people in the Bible expressed their kindness by doing good and helpful things for others. Tabitha was a well-loved member of the church in Joppa. She was known for her kindness, especially for sewing clothing for the poor.

In the city of Joppa there was a follower named Tabitha...She was always doing good deeds and *kind acts*...They showed him the *shirts* and coats Tabitha had made when she was still alive. Acts 9:36-39 (NCV)

When Paul was shipwrecked, everyone made it safely to a nearby island. The islanders showed their kindness to the survivors by building a fire for them so they could warm and dry themselves.

The islanders showed us unusual *kindness*. They *built a fire* and welcomed us all because it was raining and cold. Acts 28:2 (NIV)

Over and over in the Bible, God's kindness is equated with his deeds on our behalf.

I will tell of the *kindnesses* of the Lord, the *deeds* for which he is to be praised. Isaiah 63:7 (NIV)

In fact, everything that God does reveals his kindness and his heart of compassion toward us.

The Lord is righteous in *everything* he does; he is filled with *kindness*. Psalm 145:17 (NLT)

In the Twenty-Third Psalm, David proclaims his confidence in God's kindness and his love.

Your *kindness* and love will *always* be with me *each* day of my life. Psalm 23:6 (CEV)

Why in the world does David have such confidence in God's kindness? It is because of the things that God does. David compares the things God does to take care of him with what a shepherd does to take care of his sheep. This is a word picture that was very meaningful to David because he spent many years tending sheep for his father.

You let me *rest* in fields of green grass. You lead me to *streams* of peaceful water. Psalm 23:2 (CEV)

A shepherd provides food and water for his sheep and keeps the predators at bay. He grooms them and keeps them healthy. You see, a shepherd shows his love for the sheep by his actions.

You prepare a table before me in the presence of my *enemies*. You *anoint* my head with oil. Psalm 23:5 (NIV)

➤ Kindness requires patience

Showing kindness to others requires patience. It requires you to stay the course, to see the problem through, and to be there for the person for as long as he/she needs you. No matter what you do, if your attitude is, "Let's get this over with," your actions won't be perceived as kindness.

Some things just can't be rushed. It takes a certain amount of time for crops to grow. In the same way, it takes time to work through problems and produce lasting change. Waiting is part of life, and if you want to be kind, you will be patient about it.

See how *patient* farmers are as they *wait* for their land to produce precious crops. They wait patiently for the autumn and spring rains. James 5:7 (GN)

Problems and troubles are inevitable in life. Sometimes the only way to get through them is to outlast them, to persevere, to refuse to give up, and to keep on keeping on. You see, kindness has a tough side: it doesn't give up. It perseveres, and it is patient.

> God will strengthen you with his own great power so that you *will not give up* when troubles come, but you will be *patient*. Colossians 1:11 (NCV)

Sometimes you have difficulty showing kindness to others because they annoy or irritate you. They may say stupid things or make stupid choices or have irritating habits. They may not "get" what you tell them the first time. They may have irrational fears. They may be reluctant to take responsibility for themselves. They may be inconsistent in their behavior. Dealing with them may totally exasperate you.

But God may have put you in that situation to be his hand to them. Perhaps you are obligated to them by ties of family or work or church. You need to keep your cool. You need to be able to overlook their shortcomings and keep your eye on the goal. You need to be patient.

> Be *patient* with each other, making *allowance* for each other's faults because of your love. Ephesians 4:2 (NLT)

Patient people are humble people. They aren't full of themselves. They don't have to build themselves up by pulling others down. They can be patient and make allowance for the faults of others because they are secure in themselves. You see, humble people are patient people, but prideful people are always impatient. They are too self-absorbed to focus on the needs of others.

> *Patience* is better than too much *pride*. Ecclesiastes 7:8 (CEV)

Treat Others with Respect

One of the most attractive things about love is that it has good manners. It is never rude or disrespectful. Love always treats others with respect.

> (Love) is not *rude*. 1 Corinthians 13:5 (NIV)

Having a respectful attitude toward others is absolutely essential if you want to love them. You see, there have probably been situations in which you *said* all the right things and *did* all the right things but your attitude was all wrong. And you were anything but loving. You may have been surly or condescending or mean-spirited. But whatever your attitude was, it kept you from showing love to others.

Sometimes all it takes is a change in the inflection of your voice or the expression on your face to change the meaning of your words. Similarly, making loud noises (like slamming the door) or using jerky motions (like shoving things around) while you work can totally change the emotional meaning of your actions. You may maintain deniability, but no one is fooled. Others will feel your rejection and displeasure, and God certainly won't be pleased with your performance.

Love requires that you do the *right* thing with the *right* attitude. And the right attitude is respect for others.

➤ Treat everyone with respect

There is a respect that is *earned* by continued good or exemplary behavior. This is the respect of trust. In fact, before you trust someone with something important to you, he/she should have earned your respect in that area.

Each of you should try to live your life in such a way that you earn this kind of respect. Unfortunately, this is the only kind of respect that "takers" are willing to give others, and even then, it is often given grudgingly.

> Make it your aim to live a quiet life, to mind your own business, and to earn your own living, just as we told you before. In this way you will *win the respect* of those who are not believers. 1 Thessalonians 4:11-12 (GN)

There is also a respect that is *given*, regardless of whether the person has earned your respect or not. This is the respect of love. You see, love treats others with respect simply because God loves them. And the "givers" of this world give this kind of respect freely to others.

> Show respect for *everyone*. 1 Peter 2:17 (NLT)

God wants you to show respect for everyone, whether or not the person deserves to be respected, whether they are good or bad, and whether they treat you well or are rude and inconsiderate. There are no exceptions and no extenuating circumstances. Real love shows respect to everyone, regardless of their personal merit.

> Servants, you must obey your masters and always show *respect* to them. Do this, not only to those who are kind and thoughtful, but also to those who are *cruel.* 1 Peter 2:18 (CEV)

Respect is a key issue in marriage because each of you will make mistakes, and each of you will blow it from time to time. In those times when your spouse blows it, you need to respond to him/her in a respectful way.

You see, showing respect to others when they have blown it is like throwing them a lifeline. Your respect can help them recover and change for the better. But if you treat them disrespectfully, they will likely dig their heels in and refuse to admit their mistakes.

> Wives, be submissive to your own husbands so that even if any of them are disobedient to the word, they may be *won without a word* by the behavior of their wives, as they observe your chaste and *respectful* behavior. 1 Peter 3:1-2 (NAS)

Some of you may find that it is easier to show respect in some situations than in others. For example, a man may love and show respect to his wife when they are alone, but when he gets together with his friends he may adopt a macho banter that is disrespectful to her. Or perhaps your workplace culture is one of rudeness, one-upmanship, and "locker room" language. You may find yourself speaking to your coworkers with disrespect and insults as a matter of habit.

But God wants you to be consistent in showing respect. He wants you to show respect to everyone *everywhere.*

➤ Value others because God values them

Incredibly, God values each and every one of us. Your life, your hopes, and your disappointments matter to God. He cares about what is going on in your life. No matter who you are or what you have done, you matter to God, and you are worth something to him. In fact, he knows you so intimately that he has numbered the hairs of your head!

Five sparrows are sold for only two pennies, and God does not forget any of them. But God even knows how many *hairs* you have on your *head*. Don't be afraid. You are worth *much more* than many sparrows. Luke 12:6-7 (NCV)

When you fail to show respect for others not only are you insulting them, you are insulting God himself! When your words strip away the dignity of others, you are showing contempt for that which God loves. When your actions make others feel diminished and unappreciated, you are putting yourself in opposition to God because you are devaluing that which he values.

If you make fun of poor people, you *insult* the God who *made* them. You will be punished if you take pleasure in someone's misfortune. Proverbs 17:5 (GN)

Conversely, when you treat others with respect and kindness, you show your deep respect for God.

If you mistreat the poor, you *insult* your Creator; if you are kind to them, you show him *respect*. Proverbs 14:31 (CEV)

Those of you who are "takers" need to stop demanding that others meet your imaginary standards before you treat them with respect. Out of respect for God, you need to show others the same kind of respect that God shows to you. You see, no matter how badly you have messed up and no matter how far you have fallen short, God still treats you with consideration and respect when you come to him. You still matter to him. He still values you. He still has time for you.

Out of *respect* for *Christ*, be courteously reverent to *one another*. Ephesians 5:21 (Mes)

Each of us moves through life with these unspoken cries, "Do You Respect Me? Do I matter to you? Do I have any worth in your eyes? Do you in any way honor and esteem who I really am?" Love answers those questions in the affirmative by treating others with respect.

> ### Show appreciation for the work of others

One important way to show respect for others is to acknowledge the work they do for you with gratitude. You must never diminish those who serve you as though they were less valuable than you are. You should acknowledge their presence and their accomplishments with courtesy—not treat them as inanimate objects, as if they were machines without hopes or feelings. You should treat them with respect.

> Now we ask you, brothers, to *respect* those who *work hard* among you. 1 Thessalonians 5:12 (NIV)

You should never become so accustomed to the work of others that you begin to take what they do for you and the benefits they provide for granted. When someone is faithful and consistent in their service, they should be praised all the more. However, the unfortunate tendency in many marriages and in much of life is that people simply stop noticing and stop expressing appreciation for others' faithful service.

The very nature of living in a home together and raising children means that you each will do the same things over and over, day in and day out. Don't fall into the habit of taking the mundane tasks that your spouse does for granted. After a few years, it is very easy to stop appreciating your spouse's work to provide income, clean the house, prepare nutritious meals, pay the bills, wash the laundry, and later on, change diapers, wipe noses, clean up messes, and help with homework. All the little things (and the not so little things) that your spouse does to build your life together deserve to be recognized.

> They *refreshed* my spirit and yours also. Such men deserve *recognition*. 1 Corinthians 16:18 (NIV)

In addition, you need to see the *significance* of their service. Most of the mundane tasks your spouse does for you and your family aren't done because they are intrinsically interesting and fulfilling in and of themselves. Not at all. You see, those mundane tasks are performed in order to help you meet your larger goals in marriage, whether that be taking care of each other, raising godly children, providing a home that is a refuge from the world, or any other goal you and your spouse have chosen.

And so in expressing appreciation for your spouse's service, you should connect that service to your larger spiritual goals. You see, if you really want to make people feel valued, honored, and respected, you will recognize not just their actions but the significance of those actions.

Shortly before Jesus' death, a woman poured a very expensive perfume on his head. There was a somewhat predictable outcry from the disciples that she had wasted a large amount of money that would have been better spent on the poor.

> While Jesus was in Bethany in the home of a man known as Simon the Leper, a woman came to him with an alabaster jar of very expensive *perfume*, which she poured on his *head* as he was reclining at the table. Matthew 26:6-7 (NIV)

But Jesus rebuked the outcry by calling attention to the significance of the woman's action. You see, while everyone else was still in denial about Jesus' death, here was a woman who found a way to show him that she loved him and believed what he said.

> For when she poured this perfume on My body, she did it to *prepare* Me for *burial.* Matthew 26:12 (NAS)

➤ Keep your promises to others

When you tell others that you will do something, you need to respect them enough to do it. You see, when you promise something you set the expectations of the persons to whom you make the promise. But when you break your promise, you demonstrate that you don't care about their feelings of disappointment, and that their time, their needs, and their trust mean nothing to you. Breaking your promise devalues and diminishes them and shows a lack of respect.

> People who *promise* things that they never give are like clouds and wind that *bring no rain.* Proverbs 25:14 (GN)

"Givers" keep their promises because they are motivated by the well-being of others. But "takers" are too self-absorbed to worry (or sometimes even to notice) when they break a promise. If you are one who tends not to take promises seriously, here are some things that you can do.

First, be careful about saying things that set up expectations in others. If you say, "Let's do this again," you have set someone's expectation of a future action, even if in your mind you were just making pleasant conversation. If you say, "I'll call you tomorrow," then that person has a reasonable expectation that you will call, even if you just say those words by habit as a way of saying goodbye. If you say, "Let's go fishing next weekend," then you have made concrete plans with someone, even if you just meant that that would be a nice thing to do someday.

The words you speak to others mean something to them. When you are careless with your words, you end up making promises to others that you never intended to make or keep. When you do that you diminish the other person, and you diminish his/her trust in you.

> But I tell you that men will have to give account on the day of judgment for every *careless word* they have spoken. For by your words you will be acquitted, and by your words you will be condemned. Matthew 12:36-37 (NIV)

Second, you need to plan before making a commitment and setting someone's expectation. You need to think things through. You need to check your schedule. You need to mentally map out the logistics so that you will be able to carry through on your promise.

God always keeps his promises. You can depend upon his words. And others need to be able to depend upon your words to them. You need to keep your promises.

> The Lord is *faithful* to all his *promises* and loving toward all he has made. Psalm 145:13 (NIV)

Homework
Lesson #2: Becoming a Giver

Develop a Giving Attitude

1. Which statement in this section was the most helpful to you? Why?

2. Which of the scripture verses quoted in this section is your favorite? Why?

3. Ask your beloved: When are you a "taker"? When are you a "giver"?

DINNER TAKER

DISHES GIVER

4. Which makes you happiest: giving the gift or receiving it?

Be a Good Listener

5. Which statement in this section was the most helpful to you? Why?

6. Which of the scripture verses quoted in this section is your favorite? Why?

7. Do you enjoy conversation or do you prefer silence? Why?

8. What nonverbal clues does your beloved give when sad? When upset?

Show Kindness to Others

9. Which statement in this section was the most helpful to you? Why?

10. Which of the scripture verses quoted in this section is your favorite? Why?

11. Ask your beloved: how quick are you to understand someone else's point of view?

12. Ask your beloved: are you quick to become impatient or frustrated?

Treat Others with Respect

13. Which statement in this section was the most helpful to you? Why?

14. Which of the scripture verses quoted in this section is your favorite? Why?

15. Ask your beloved: are you respectful toward people who blow it?

16. Have you and your beloved had a misunderstanding because one of you made an offhand comment that the other took as a commitment? Please explain.

Lesson #3: Overcoming Selfishness

Love isn't *selfish*. 1 Corinthians 13:5 (CEV)

Love focuses on *others*; it looks outward beyond yourself to the other people in your world. Love thinks of what others need, how they feel, and how events impact them.

In contrast, selfishness focuses on *yourself*; you are the center of your own universe. It looks inward, being preoccupied with what you need, how you feel, and how external events impact you. At best, it is simply indifferent to the needs of the other people in your world. At its worst, it is cruelly manipulative of others.

Selfishness and love are opposites. You cannot be selfish and loving at the same time. If your thoughts are selfish, you will not be able to act with love. But when your thoughts are full of love, you will act unselfishly. It is axiomatic.

So if you want to grow in love for your beloved, you must guard against selfishness. Selfishness will undercut everything you try to do concerning love. It will make a mockery of the things you try to do and to say to express your love. It will make you a liar and a fake. Selfishness will keep you from being able to demonstrate real love to your beloved.

Worse still, your selfishness will slowly kill the love your spouse has for you. You see, relationships are not self-perpetuating; they have to be tended and nourished on a regular basis. The reciprocal nature of marriage necessitates that each spouse nourish the other with loving words, kind deeds, and respectful attitudes.

Be *devoted to one another* in brotherly love. Honor one another above yourselves. Romans 12:10 (NIV)

When selfishness keeps you from nourishing your beloved, your marriage slowly starves to death! If you do not nourish your spouse, your spouse's love for you will eventually run out—no matter how committed he/she is to loving you. And so when you find yourself thinking, "This marriage is getting kind of stale," you need to ask yourself whether your attitudes, words, and deeds are being motivated by selfishness.

The Fallacy of Pride

> Love is not jealous or *boastful* or *proud*. 1 Corinthians 13:4 (NLT)

A lot of selfish behavior is driven by pride. You see, prideful people think only of themselves in the things they do and say. They are arrogant and overbearing and seem to have an exaggerated opinion of themselves. They are unable to nurture those around them because they feel compelled to draw everything back to themselves, to affirm how truly wonderful or powerful they are.

Ironically, prideful people don't really think they are as wonderful as they want you to believe they are. Prideful people are actually very insecure people; they have a very fragile sense of their own self-worth. Therefore, they continually draw attention to themselves in an effort to prove that they are competent, successful, talented, beautiful—whatever it is that makes them feel valuable.

Prideful people try to cover up their insecurities with arrogance and boasting. They tend to be very critical of others. They try to build themselves up by tearing others down.

> We have endured much *ridicule* from the proud, much *contempt* from the arrogant. Psalm 123:4 (NIV)

The fallacy of pride is that it can never build the sense of self-worth that the prideful person so desperately seeks. Pride will always fail as a life strategy because you can never accumulate enough accomplishments, enough wealth, enough adulation, enough success, enough knowledge, enough power, or enough prestige to build a stable sense of self-worth. You see, your value and your uniqueness come from God.

➢ Having to be the best

The fallacy of pride is thinking that you only have value if you're the best at something. Pride assumes that weaknesses are something to be ashamed of. As a result, you will be deceived by your pride. You will overestimate your strengths and underestimate your weaknesses.

Your *pride* has *deceived* you. No one fears you as much as you think they do.
Jeremiah 49:16 (GN)

But the real danger of pride is not understanding that God has created you
with a unique "shape." Your strengths *and* your weaknesses are both part of the
package that makes you able to fulfill the purposes God has for your life. When
you are humble, you can be honest about both your strengths and your weaknesses because you understand that God is the one who created you that way.

Be *honest* in your estimate of *yourselves*. Romans 12:3 (NLT)

Remember, God is able to use even your weaknesses!

But to keep me from being *puffed* up with *pride*…I was given a painful physical ailment…Three times I prayed to the Lord about this and asked him to
take it away. But his answer was: "My grace is all you need, for my *power* is
greatest when you are *weak*." 2 Corinthians 12:7-9 (GN)

You see, Paul had received astounding revelations from God. But to keep
them from becoming a point of pride for him, God gave him a "thorn in the
flesh" to remind him of his human weakness—and his total dependence upon
God. God works through your weaknesses as well as your strengths. Wow.

➤ Having to be in control

The fallacy of pride is thinking that being powerful makes you valuable. And
so the prideful person seeks to control everything and everyone in his/her world.

One of the keys to overcoming selfishness is to learn to relinquish control over
things in your life. It is learning to let others make choices about what to watch
on TV, where to go for dinner, what car to buy, what movie to see, when to go to
bed, and how long to visit the in-laws.

Even more important is learning to let God be in control. You see, God has
good plans for you; he wants to direct your steps for your benefit.

"I know what I am *planning* for you," says the Lord. "I have good plans for
you, not plans to hurt you. I will give you *hope* and a good *future*." Jeremiah
29:11 (NCV)

But the prideful person wants to make his own plans and to be in control of his own destiny. After setting his own course, he comes to God and expects God to bless the plans he has made for himself. This is a very prideful attitude toward God. You see, if you want God's blessing, you need to come to God first and ask him for direction. Then as you follow his direction, you can be confident that God will bless your steps.

> With God's *power* working in us, God can do much, *much more* than anything we can ask or imagine. Ephesians 3:20 (NCV)

God's ways are always best. We can be confident of the direction that God sets for us, but we must learn to trust him.

Mary the mother of Jesus is a beautiful example of trusting God. Mary had her plans. She was engaged to Joseph, and they probably had their lives all planned out. But Gabriel, God's messenger angel, showed up on her doorstep one day. He told her that God was pleased with her, and that she would conceive and have a son who would be *God's* son, the promised Messiah. Although she had her own plans, she was willing to put them aside to do whatever God wanted.

> Mary said, "I am the Lord's servant! Let it *happen* as you have *said*." Luke 1:38 (CEV)

➢ Trying to have it all

The fallacy of pride is thinking that your achievements make you valuable. Prideful people try to "have it all," do it all, and be it all in a desperate effort to prove their worth to themselves and others. But the effort to prove your worth by your achievements is doomed from the start. Unlike God, you are a limited being. There are limits to what you can do and be and have. You have to make choices and set priorities in your life.

In this day and age it is very easy to get into a performance trap. However, trying to "have it all" will only leave you worn out, exhausted, tired, and stressed out. You will be stressed out because you're trying to do more than God created you to do. You need to understand your limitations, and that nobody can have it all. You see, whenever it looks like someone "has it all," you can be sure that you don't know the whole story.

One way to understand your limitations is to embrace God's plan for you. God's plan will give your life focus and help you set priorities. Moreover, it is tailor-made for your personality, your abilities, and your energy level.

> Take the *yoke* I give you. Put it on your shoulders and *learn* from me. I am gentle and humble, and you will find *rest*. Matthew 11:29 (CEV)

The yoke is a wooden frame that joins two oxen together at the neck so that they can pull together. Jesus is saying that when you embrace his plan for your life, it is like getting into a yoke with him. He will walk beside you, helping you pull the load, setting the pace, and establishing your direction. Your load will be easier, there will be less stress in your life, and you will have peace.

> The *humble* will possess the land and enjoy prosperity and *peace*. Psalm 37:11 (GN)

The second problem with trying to have it all is that you end up *relationally skimming*. Your schedule gets so full and your life becomes so busy that you don't have time for the most important people in your life: your spouse, your kids, and your close friends or associates. You don't have the time it takes to really invest and nurture those relationships, to be there for them when it matters, to really listen to them, and to share your heart with them. You're just going through the motions in these relationships. You're not nurturing them; you're just living off fumes from the past.

Having time for those you love is an important part of loving them. If you aren't available to them when they need you, then you have let them down. Child psychiatrist James Dobson is fond of saying, "Kids spell love T-I-M-E."[1] If you want to grow in love, you will have to set priorities in your life.

➢ Having to know it all

The fallacy of pride is thinking that not knowing something diminishes your value as a person. Prideful people are unwilling to learn from others. They need to keep up their façade of "knowing it all" in order to prop up their fragile sense of self-worth. If they must learn something, they are only willing to listen to those who are suitably qualified and certified—those whom they consider their equals or betters. Prideful people are snobs.

If you think about it though, everybody is ignorant about something, and everybody has some area of expertise. God has given us different areas of expertise so that we can work together just like the different parts of your physical body work together. Our areas of expertise complement one another.

> Just as our bodies have *many* parts and each part has a *special function*, so it is with Christ's body. We are all parts of his one body, and each of us has *different* work to do. Romans 12:4-5 (NLT)

We need to learn from each other. In fact, God says that we should model the humility of a little child. Babies and little children are eager to learn. They are aggressive learners, and they are willing to learn from *anyone*.

> Anyone who becomes as *humble* as this little *child* is the greatest in the Kingdom of Heaven. Matthew 18:4 (NLT)

Now one of the most important things you can do to learn from others is to ask them questions. You see, humble people ask questions so they can learn from others, but prideful people don't. They can't afford to admit to themselves or others that they don't know something.

Prideful people are also unwilling to learn from God. It unbalances their fragile sense of self-esteem to have to admit that God is God and they aren't, that he knows better than they do, and that there are things they need to change about their lives. You see, God wants to teach you his ways, and he uses the circumstances of your life to do so.

> He took away your *pride* when he let you get *hungry*, and then he fed you with *manna*, which neither you nor your ancestors had ever seen. This was to *teach you* that a person does not live by eating only bread, but by everything the Lord says. Deuteronomy 8:3 (NCV)

You see, in whatever circumstance you find yourself, you need to ask God, "What are you trying to say to me, and what do you want to teach me in this?"

> With *humility* comes *wisdom*. Proverbs 11:2 (NLT)

➢ **Always having to be right**

The fallacy of pride is thinking that making mistakes diminishes your value as a person. Prideful people refuse to admit when they are wrong about something.

They refuse to take responsibility for their mistakes. They are quick to point the finger at someone else when something goes wrong.

Moreover, when prideful people are confronted with overwhelming evidence of their missteps, they issue vague and unsatisfying apologies, such as, "If *anyone* was offended by *what happened*, I'm sorry." Such apologies are really a back-handed slap at the wounded parties for being overly sensitive. It is in no way an admission of guilt.

> A man who refuses to *admit* his *mistakes* can never be successful. Proverbs 28:13 (LB)

This is because prideful people confuse their actions with their *worth* as an individual. They think that if you make a mistake, it makes you a bad person—that your person as well as your action is blameworthy. Fortunately, that is not the way God thinks about you. He may detest your failure, but he never stops loving you. Jesus unequivocally hates the sin, but he deeply loves the sinner.

> "Why does your teacher eat with tax collectors and *sinners*?" On hearing this, Jesus said, "It is not the healthy who need a doctor, but the sick…For I have not *come* to call the righteous, but *sinners*." Matthew 9:11-13 (NIV)

The truth of the matter is that we all fail regularly in our lives. Flops, fumbles, and failures are inevitable. They don't make you a bad person, but they do make you a person who needs to admit that you were wrong. And if someone was harmed by your action, you need to ask them to forgive you. Because of Jesus you don't have to be right all the time, but you do need to make things right when you fail.

Growing up you may never have heard the words, "I was wrong. I'm sorry. Will you forgive me?" As a result, you may have a very hard time coming clean because no one modeled this behavior for you. But no matter how you grew up, you can change your ways.

> But if he *confesses* and forsakes (his mistakes), he gets another *chance*. Proverbs 28:13 (LB)

The interesting thing about admitting your mistakes is that, instead of people thinking less of you because of your mistakes, they think more of you because you admitted them. You see, when you are honest about your mistakes, and you don't try to candy coat what you've done, God gives you a second chance to make things right.

> ## Needing to defend yourself

The fallacy of pride is thinking that false accusations diminish your value as a person. Prideful people are quick to defend themselves. They are quick to argue their own point of view, and they are quick to seek vindication.

However, when someone is hurting, and when they are speaking out of their hurt and confusion, trying to jump in and defend yourself is like pouring gasoline on a fire. It just makes things worse. What is needed is for you to listen to them as they try to sort out their thoughts and their feelings.

Moreover, if someone has an honest disagreement with you, repeating your point of view over and over again will not help you resolve your disagreement. On the contrary, it will just inflame passions. You will never be able to resolve your disagreement until you understand the other person's point of view, and you will never understand his/her point of view until you really listen to him/her. Understanding each other's point of view brings respect to your discussion, helps you find common ground, and allows you to explore possible solutions or alternatives.

> *Pride* only leads to *arguments*, but those who take *advice* are wise. Proverbs 13:10 (NCV)

Here's a tough one. How do you respond to unjust criticism? Do you show respect to the other person by listening to them without interruption? Do you ask honest questions in an attempt to understand their point of view? Are you argumentative with them, or do you try to help them solve their problem? Are you thinking about yourself, or are you concerned about them? You see, sometimes the criticism isn't really about you at all.

But if the criticism is deserved, and if someone is trying to bring correction and balance into your life, how do you receive them? Are you argumentative and defensive, or are you willing to listen with an open mind? Do you see their words as a personal attack, or do you see them as an opportunity to learn and grow, to get rid of a problem that is hurting you and others?

> If you *reject* criticism, you only harm yourself; but if you *listen* to correction you grow in *understanding*. Proverbs 15:32 (NLT)

When someone offers correction, you have a choice to make. Will you try to defend yourself or will you accept the correction? You see, in most situations it is possible to offer some sort of defense for your actions. However, if you do so, you won't learn what God wants you to learn. You see, defensiveness never gets you where you need to go. It only leads to further conflict.

> Those who *listen* to *instruction* will prosper; those who trust the Lord will be happy. Proverbs 16:20 (NLT)

The prideful person always has turf to defend. Because of self-centeredness, he/she views everything as a personal attack. But the humble person doesn't have turf to defend. He can listen with an open mind, he can bring healing to the hurting, and he can learn from his mistakes. And in so doing, he will gain wisdom and respect.

> *Pride* leads to *destruction*; humility leads to *honor*. Proverbs 18:12 (CEV)

The Fallacy of Envy

> (Love) does not envy. 1 Corinthians 13:4 (NIV)

A lot of selfish behavior is driven by envy. You see, envious people can only enjoy good things when they happen to themselves; they cannot enjoy the good things that happen to others. It never occurs to them to be concerned about the needs, the hopes, the hurts, and the disappointments of others—or to put someone else's well-being before their own. In fact, envious people resent it when good things happen to others, especially if they want those same things for themselves.

Envious people are so preoccupied with what they want and so controlled by their disappointment in not getting it, that they withdraw into their own little world to throw a Pity Party for themselves. "Poor little ol' me!" They are masters at nursing their hurts, their disappointments, their resentments, and their bitterness. Envious people are doomed to be unhappy people and to make those around them unhappy, too.

➤ Seeking happiness from external thing

The fallacy of envy is thinking that happiness comes from your possessions, your accomplishments, your relationships, your circumstances—the external things of your life. However, the things envious people think they need in order to be happy can never make them happy, because happiness is always a moving target for them. Whatever they already have, they always need more to be happy.

> Those who love money will *never* have *enough*. How absurd to think that wealth brings true happiness! Ecclesiastes 5:10 (NLT)

Happiness doesn't come from the external circumstances of your life; it comes from inside you. It reflects how you feel about your relationship with God and with yourself. It reflects your contentment with what you have now and your hope for the future. You see, happiness comes from within.

> He who believes in Me, as the Scripture said, 'From his *innermost being* will flow rivers of *living water*.' John 7:38 (NAS)

Driving a certain car or living in a certain house or having a certain job won't make you happy. Getting married won't make you happy if you weren't happy before. Getting rid of a certain annoying co-worker or taking a romantic vacation or moving to a new neighborhood won't make you happy. You see, if you're not happy with yourself and if you don't trust God, changing your possessions, your accomplishments, your relationships, or your circumstances won't make any difference. Happiness will continue to elude you.

Because our economy is consumer driven, you are subjected to unrelenting messages everywhere to "have it *all* and have it now." As a result, you find yourself wanting things you never knew you wanted and rationalizing how you really need them after all. Envy takes root when you see others with the things you want, and you begin thinking, "I want what they have, I want more than they have, and I want it *now*."

> It's healthy to be *content*, but *envy* can eat you up. Proverbs 14:30 (CEV)

There is a lot of truth to the old saying, "Folks are just about as happy as they make up their minds to be," because happiness isn't dependent upon your external circumstances.

➤ Comparing your situation to others'

The fallacy of envy is thinking that your situation is comparable to someone else's. God has shaped you as a unique individual. No one is exactly like you. No one has the exact same mix of talent, intellect, and interests. No one has your background or your unique set of experiences. No one has the hopes and dreams that you do.

> We will not *compare* ourselves with each other as if one of us were better and another worse. We have far more interesting things to do with our lives. Each of us is an *original*. Galatians 5:26 (Mes)

So, comparing your situation with someone else's is like trying to compare apples and oranges—they are too different to make meaningful comparisons.

God's plan for you is unique. God has a unique race for you to run in life—a particular contribution that only you can make. God has a purpose for your life that is custom crafted to make expert use of who you are and what you have experienced in your life. Therefore, the training God gives you for your race will also be unique; it will be different from the training he gives someone else for their race.

> Let us *run* with patience the *particular* race that God has set before us. Hebrews 12:1 (LB)

Furthermore, God blesses us in different ways. God blesses some with good health; some with a good family life, some with good achievements, and some with great wealth. The blessings you receive from God are uniquely crafted to fulfill God's purpose for your life, to form you into the person he has created you to be, and to meet your needs and the needs of others.

> *Grace* is given to us in *different* ways out of the rich diversity of Christ's giving. Ephesians 4:7 (JBP)

Finally, comparisons are faulty because you seldom know the whole story behind what you think others have. You don't understand the sacrifice, the pain, and the emotional turmoil that are part of their lives. When you see someone from a distance, you only see their successes and their status. It is only when you get close to them that you see their problems and their failures. You see, no one ever "has it all." Nobody is ever as happy or as satisfied or as carefree as they seem to be. And so comparisons with others are faulty because you always end up comparing their successes against your failures.

➢ Competing with others for God's blessings

The fallacy of envy is thinking that you must compete with everyone else for God's blessings. It's thinking that God's blessings to others reduce his blessings to you. As a result, the envious person resents the good things that happen in the lives of other people.

You see, the economy of envy is the economy of scarcity: there aren't enough good things to go around. The envious person thinks of life as a Zero Sum Game, where if someone gets more of something, someone else necessarily gets less. Think of dividing up an apple pie between eight people; a large slice for one person means smaller slices for everyone else.

No wonder the envious person sees himself/herself in competition with everyone else. In his/her world, when someone wins, someone else has to lose. Envy is motivated by the fear of being left out, of not getting enough, or of not getting what everyone else is getting.

The fallacy of envy is thinking that God has a limited number of blessings he can bestow. This is absurd. God is infinite, and the blessings he can bestow are infinite, too. God has more than enough blessings for everyone.

> "Test Me now in this," says the Lord of hosts, "if I will not open for you the windows of heaven and pour out for you a *blessing* until it *overflows*. Malachi 3:10 (NAS)

Do you see how selfish envy is? It is focusing on yourself to the exclusion of others and their needs. It is resenting God's goodness to others because you think that it somehow takes away from what you need or deserve. Envy cares only for itself.

But generosity is focused on others. It cares about the well-being of others. It shares their hopes and dreams. It seeks to meet their needs, and to be their advocate and their cheerleader. The generous person believes that when someone is blessed, *everyone* is made richer.

> *Rejoice* with those who *rejoice*! Romans 12:15 (NAS)

When God is blessing someone else, you need to be happy for them. You need to put aside your own disappointments and focus instead on God's goodness.

When God's demonstrates his goodness to others you shouldn't feel threatened or left out. You should be filled with hope, and your faith should be stirred. You see, when God meets a need for someone else, it demonstrates that he is *able* to meet your need, also. When he blesses others, it demonstrates that he *wants* to bless you, too.

> Now to Him who is *able* to do far *more abundantly* beyond all that we ask or think... Ephesians 3:20 (NAS)

➢ Focusing on your disappointments

The fallacy of envy is focusing on your disappointments instead of your blessings. Envious people always ignore the blessings they have already received; they fixate instead on what they thought they deserved but didn't get. Envy dwells on your disappointments and the negative aspects of your life.

The focus of your envy is always the person who has more than you do, not the person who has less. Envy always chooses a standard of comparison that allows you to nurse your hurts and your sense of entitlement. But what if your standard of comparison was with someone who has less than you do—who is less well off than you are? Wow. That would change your attitude really fast.

You see, the antidote to envy is gratitude. If you want to root envy out of your life, you need to learn to be grateful for the things you *do* have. If you tried to list everything in your life that was good, could you do it? Could you ever complete the list? Probably not, but the process of trying would change your attitude. It would certainly help you to put your disappointments into perspective.

> Whatever is *good* and perfect comes to us *from God* above. James 1:17 (NLT)

If you are struggling with envy, you need to develop a habit of thanksgiving. Every good thing in your life was put there by God. He loves you, and he delights in blessing you. He also delights in hearing you thank him for his gifts.

What is more, you need to thank God for your blessings more than God needs to hear your thanks. Thanking God is a transformational process that changes your attitude and stirs your faith.

> Sing and make music in your heart to the Lord, *always giving thanks* to God the Father for everything. Ephesians 5:19-20 (NIV)

No situation in your life is without God's blessings if you will learn to look for them. No matter how great your disappointment, and no matter how bleak your circumstances, God has placed an abundance of his blessing and his mercy there for you. If you focus on your disappointment, though, you will miss the good things God is doing in your life.

> Be *joyful* always; pray continually; give *thanks* in *all circumstances*, for this is God's will for you in Christ Jesus. 1 Thessalonians 5:16-18 (NIV)

➤ Confusing your needs with your wants

The fallacy of envy is thinking that you really need the things you want. There is a big difference between what is adequate to meet your basic needs of food, clothing, shelter, transportation, education, and employment *and* the standard of living that you'd like to have.

Moreover, your standard of living is a moving target which is always being revised upward. It is very easy to justify the luxuries you already have as things you need. In fact, the human heart has an amazing ability to rationalize why you need to have certain things, and how certain luxuries actually meet needs that you have. The fact is, you can justify almost anything you want to yourself as a need.

> It is better to be *satisfied* with what you *have* than to be always wanting something else. Ecclesiastes 6:9 (GN)

Lots of couples get into financial difficulties, running up huge debts and arguing about money, because they have lost sight of the difference between their needs and their wants. They feel justified in buying something they want but can't afford.

Now the point isn't that you should never have nice things or that you should never have more than you need. The point is that when you do have more than you need, you should recognize it and enjoy those things as the luxuries they are—as tokens of God's goodness to you.

Happiness comes from enjoying what you already have, not in getting more of whatever it is you want. After all, if the things you already have don't bring you happiness, the things you think you want won't bring you happiness either. Therefore, contentment is an important antidote to envy. Learning to appreciate and fully enjoy what you have now will still the fires of envy that rage within you. You'll be much happier in your life.

> I have *learned* to be *content* whatever the circumstances. Philippians 4:11 (NIV)

God promises to supply all your needs, but he never promises to supply all your wants. He's not some slot machine into which you can throw a couple of quarters, say a couple of prayers, pull down the crank, and out comes anything you want.

> My God will use his wonderful riches in Christ Jesus to give you *everything* you *need*. Philippians 4:19 (NCV)

You see, God's primary purpose is to develop your character so that you become more like him. And sometimes the situations you like the least are the ones that develop your character the most. Sometimes the best thing for you is not to get that thing you want so badly. Sometimes God has a much better plan than the one you have for yourself. On the other hand, sometimes you will eventually get the thing you really want, but God wants you to grow up a little first.

> I have learned the secret of being *content* in any and every situation...whether living in plenty or in want. I can do everything *through him* who gives me strength. Philippians 4:12-13 (NIV)

➢ Doubting God's goodness

The fallacy of envy is thinking that God's goodness means you will always get what you want. Envious people want to dictate the terms of their happiness to God, instead of finding happiness in the unique plan that God has for them.

When you envy the person who has something you want but didn't get, your beef isn't really with the person you envy; your beef is with God. You are accusing God of being unfair. You are doubting God's goodness in withholding what you want. You are resisting God's plan for your life. You see, when you are envious, you are really in a battle with God. Wow.

Whenever life seems unfair, you need to step back, take a deep breath, and trust God that he knows exactly what he is doing and that he is still in control. The antidote for envy is trusting God that he is working for your good even when you don't understand the circumstances you find yourself in.

> We know that *in everything* God works for the *good* of those who love him. Romans 8:28 (NCV)

Do you want more joy in your life? You don't need more things, you need to trust God. Do you want more peace in your life? You don't need what you think you want; you need to trust God more. Do you want to be filled with hope for the future? Then you need to trust God that he is working through the circumstances of your life to bring you a better future.

> May the God of hope fill you with all *joy* and *peace* as you *trust* in him, so that you may overflow with *hope* by the power of the Holy Spirit. Romans 15:13 (NIV)

Envy is a sign that you have fallen out of love with God. It is a sign that God is no longer at the center of your life, that getting to know him better no longer fuels your passions, and that your thoughts and your hopes are no longer formed by his Word. Envy is a warning sign that your life has gotten badly out of focus, and that you need to rekindle the love that you have for God.

> But this is what I have against you: you do not *love* me now as you did *at first*. Revelation 2:4 (GN)

The Habit of Unselfishness

Some people are by their natural bent more selfish than others; others of you are naturally unselfish. Some people are naturally wired to consider others in their thoughts; others of you aren't. Some of you are aware of what those around you are thinking and feeling, while some of you wouldn't have a clue even if they were trying to tell you.

In any marriage one of the partners will be more selfish than the other. And if you aren't careful, it can make for big problems, and big imbalances, in your marriage. You see, if you are the more selfish one in your marriage, you need to be very aggressive about acting in unselfish ways or you will run your marriage into the ground. Your selfishness can starve your marriage to death almost before you notice anything is wrong.

> When you do things, do not let *selfishness* or pride be your guide. Instead, be humble and *give* more honor to *others* than to yourselves. Philippians 2:3 (NCV)

Having said that, every single one of us needs to grow in unselfishness. In fact, one of the benefits of marriage is that it is a built-in laboratory to help you grow in unselfishness. You see, living in marriage will expose selfishness in your heart that you didn't know was there. The realities of day-to-day living in the unique closeness of marriage give you lots of opportunities to practice acting unselfishly.

> The things you have *learned* and received and heard and seen in me, *practice* these things, and the God of peace will be with you. Philippians 4:9 (NAS)

Unselfishness, like all Christian virtues, is learned through practice. You begin by making a conscious choice to think in a certain way about something or to take a certain action. It may seem a little forced or unnatural to you at first, but if you repeat that conscious decision over and over and over, it eventually becomes your habit.

➤ Focus on others

One of the most devastating things about selfishness is that it never even occurs to you to think of anyone else. It never occurs to you how someone might feel about what you're saying, how they might be affected by what you're doing, or what their needs might be in the situation. You are just tooling along in your own little world, thinking of yourself, and considering everything from your own point of view.

God says to get the focus off yourself and onto others. You need to make a conscious choice as you begin your day to pray, "Help me to notice other people today. Help me to be aware of their needs as well as my own."

> Don't think only about your *own* affairs, but be *interested* in *others*, too. Philippians 2:4 (NLT)

As you are making a decision, you need to ask yourself, "How would these various options affect the other people in my world? What option would be best for them?"

When you become aware that you are tired or hungry or bored or emotionally spent, you need to stop and look around. You need to ask yourself, "Are there other people who feel the same way I do right now? What can I do to meet their needs as well as my own?"

> For I am not seeking my *own* good but the good of *many*, so that they may be saved. 1 Corinthians 10:33 (NIV)

When you have an urge to tell someone about your day, stop for a moment, and ask them about their day instead. You see, one of the best ways to learn about what someone is thinking or feeling, what they are doing, or the problems they are having, is simply to listen to them as they talk.

Make a conscious choice to really listen to them—to put your whole focus on the person who is speaking *and* to pay attention to what they are saying and the meaning it has for them. Whatever you do, don't use the time they are talking to formulate what you are going to say next. And don't assume that a pause in the conversation is your invitation to jump in and start talking.

➤ Give preference to others

Some of you are natural competitors. While there are strengths in that (such as courage and leadership), giving preference to others isn't one of your strong suits. In fact, it is downright unnatural for you to do so. You will intentionally have to choose to give preference to others.

> Don't be obsessed with getting your own advantage. *Forget yourselves* long enough to lend a *helping* hand. Philippians 2:4 (Mes)

Giving preference to others is about showing common courtesy to others: letting them go first, giving them the best seat, letting them take the last parking place in the lot, and letting them have the spotlight. If you want to take your courtesy up a notch, it is about making them comfortable, helping them to feel at ease in a situation, letting them know that they are valued by your actions, and giving them recognition and honor in front of others.

> Let love be without hypocrisy...Be devoted to one another in brotherly love; give *preference* to *one another* in honor. Romans 12:9-10 (NAS)

Sometimes giving preference to others is deciding that their needs take precedence over your own. It is making a conscious decision that you are going to deny yourself, that you will meet somebody else's needs at the expense of your own, and that you will indulge somebody else's wants instead of satisfying your own.

> Then Jesus said to His disciples, "If anyone wishes to come after Me, he must *deny himself*, and take up his cross and follow Me." Matthew 16:24 (NAS)

Usually life doesn't require you to make such a stark choice, but you need to be willing to make that choice if it is required. Frequently, what is needed is that you defer meeting your own need until after you have met the need of someone else. Sometimes, if you are willing to modify your plans and rethink what it is that you really want, you can come up with a plan that allows both of you to get what you want, or something even better.

To grow in love you need to learn to give preference to others. To have consistency in that love, you need to make giving preference to others your habit.

➢ Serve others

One of the unique things about Christianity is that it links greatness with service. It requires its leaders to serve those they lead.

> You know that foreign rulers like to *order* their people around…But don't act like them. If you want to be *great*, you must be the *servant* of all the others. Matthew 20:25-26 (CEV)

Everyone, regardless of their status, must serve one another because of the example Jesus set for us.

> …just as the Son of Man did not come *to be served*, but *to serve*, and to give his life as a ransom for many. Matthew 20:28 (NIV)

Now some of you are very aware of what needs to be done in a situation, but you aren't willing to get involved in the grunt work yourself. You want to bark orders, to delegate, and to get others busy meeting those needs. However, that's not service, and that's not true leadership.

The way to earn the respect of those you lead is to work alongside them, joining them in performing the lowliest of tasks. First, you need to become aware of the lowly tasks others perform for you on a routine basis. Then, you need to begin working with them to make their load lighter. For example, you can load the dishwasher when your spouse is cleaning up the kitchen after a meal. You can carry in the groceries from the car while she puts them away. You can make the bed in the morning before you go off to work. You can pick up your clothes and put them in the hamper so they will be ready to wash.

> Don't use your freedom as an excuse to do anything you want. Use it as an opportunity to *serve each other* with love. Galatians 5:13 (CEV)

Furthermore you need to make a conscious choice to do more than is expected or required of you. That means you need to take the initiative in performing acts of service, not wait to be asked. You need to volunteer for that job no one wants to do.

> If a soldier forces you to carry his pack *one* mile, carry it *two* miles. Matthew 5:41 (CEV)

There is truly something transformational about serving others out of love for the Lord. It brings freedom and joy to you personally, and it brings respect and value to those you serve.

> *Serve* wholeheartedly, as if you were serving the *Lord*, not men. Ephesians 6:7 (NIV)

Homework
Lesson #3: Overcoming Selfishness

1. What change do you need to make to better nourish your marriage?

The Fallacy of Pride

2. Which statement in this section was most helpful to you? Why?

3. Which of the scripture verses quoted in this section is your favorite? Why?

4. Do you struggle with your sense of self-worth? Why?

5. Which fallacy of pride is the greatest temptation for you personally?

The Fallacy of Envy

6. Which statement in this section was most helpful to you? Why?

7. Which of the scripture verses quoted in this section is your favorite? Why?

8. Which fallacy of envy is the greatest temptation for you personally?

9. Ask your beloved: are you a naturally competitive person?

10. In your gut, do you feel like there are enough good things to go around?

11. Ask your beloved: are you naturally pessimistic in your view of life?

12. Do you tend to focus on your disappointments or your blessings?

13. Do you spend more than you earn?

14. How clearly do you distinguish your needs from your wants?

The Habit of Unselfishness

15. Which statement in this section was most helpful to you? Why?

16. Which of the scripture verses quoted in this section is your favorite? Why?

17. Ask your beloved: is your natural bent toward selfishness?

18. Give an example of a situation in which you chose to give preference to another person.

Lesson #4: The Nature of Marriage

God Created Marriage

The most important thing you need to know about marriage is that marriage is not your own personal creation. You don't get to make up the rules as you go along. You can try, and plenty of people do, but you cannot suspend the laws of nature and of God.

God himself created marriage. Moreover, marriage was a central part of his plan, not an afterthought or some way he devised to tie up loose ends. God's plan for marriage is woven into every detail of the world he created; it is woven into every fiber of your being. Therefore, your success and happiness in marriage depend upon understanding how God created marriage to function.

> Unless the *Lord* builds the *house*, its builders labor in vain. Psalm 127:1 (NIV)

You will benefit greatly by embracing God's plan for marriage. You won't be on your own as you struggle in the adjustments of marriage and life's crises as you would be if you were making it up as you went along. You see, God has so designed marriage that as you embrace the roles he has for you, you will strengthen one another, not tear one another apart.

As you embrace the purpose God has for marriage you will find true fulfillment and contentment in your marriage. Your love for one another has brought you to marriage, but love alone cannot sustain your marriage in the years to come. Ironically, it will be your commitment to God's purpose for your marriage that will nurture and sustain your love in the coming years.

> His *power* at work in us can do *far more* than we dare ask or imagine. Ephesians 3:20 (CEV)

God's plans for your marriage are better than you could have imagined, but first you need to get on board with him.

➤ Created male and female

The Creation Story tells us two very wonderful things. First, human beings are unique because we alone of all created beings were made in God's image. God gave us the capacity to see the things he sees, to feel the things he feels, and to know the things he knows. We can have the same character he has, act with the same motives he does, and love others with the same love he shows us.

Second, although we are created in God's image, we only receive a portion of that image, not the complete package. God created human beings in two sexes—male and female, men and women—and he distributed to each sex different aspects of his character, his motives, his strength, and his creativity. You see, God's image is not adequately expressed by either maleness or femaleness. Both sets of attributes are necessary to express who God is.

> God created people in his own *image*; God patterned them after himself; *male and female* he created them. Genesis 1:27 (NLT)

Men and women need each other. They have been given different pieces of the puzzle that is life. Their strengths are different, they have different points of view, and they are sensitive to different things. If they embrace their differences and learn to depend upon each other, they will strengthen and balance one another.

> God said, "It is not good for the man to live *alone*. I will make a *suitable companion* to help him." Genesis 2:18 (GN)

The physiological differences between men and women exist in every system of the body, not just the reproductive system. Recent studies of the brain reveal that male and female brains are hard-wired differently, resulting in different perspectives, interests, and sensitivities.[1]

> Males and females, it turns out, are different from the moment of conception, and the difference shows itself in every system of body and brain...Male and female minds are innately drawn to different aspects of the world around them. Psychology Today (July/Aug 2003)

God created men and women differently because no finite being could contain God's image. By working together and letting their differences complement one another, men and women are able to present a more complete picture of God's nature that they could individually. You see, marriage is one of the ways that God reveals himself to us.

> Don't you know that in the beginning the Creator made a man and a woman? *That's why* a man leaves his father and mother and gets *married.* Matthew 19:4-5 (CEV)

➤ Joined into a functioning unit

When a man and a woman marry, they establish a family. Families were created by God to be permanent functioning units. They are the basic unit of human society, upon which the health and well-being of the community and nation depend. The Bible refers to this process of a husband and wife learning to function together in a single unit as becoming One Flesh.

> 'For this reason a man will leave his father and mother and be *united* to his wife, and the two will become *one flesh.*' So they are no longer two, but one. Mark 10:7-8 (NIV)

Becoming one in marriage doesn't mean that you cease to function as individuals or that you lose your individual identities. Not at all. After all, how could you complement one another if you lost your individual distinctiveness? Nor does it mean that you are somehow inadequate without each other or before your marriage.

Becoming one in marriage simply means that you learn to function together as a unit, that you become a team, and that you have a common purpose. Scientifically speaking, marriage is a system which is greater than the sum of its parts. There is a *synergism*[2] in marriage that makes you both better and more effective than you would be otherwise, and that enables you to take on tasks that would be impossible for you to accomplish individually.

Moreover, becoming one in marriage is multifaceted because it involves every part of your being. It involves your whole person. It unites your hearts and minds, your souls and spirits, as well as your bodies.

> May the God who gives us peace…keep your *whole being*—spirit, soul, and body—free from every fault. 1 Thessalonians 5:23 (GN)

Your happiness and contentment in marriage will depend upon the degree to which your relationship with your spouse is multifaceted. You need to develop a spiritual fellowship with one another, where you pray together and where God's word shapes the way you view your world. You need to develop a friendship with your spouse, where you talk about the things that matter most to you and gain perspective from one another. You need to develop an intellectual relationship, where you stimulate each other to learn new things and apply that knowledge in ways that enrich your life together. You need to develop an emotional sensitivity to each other, learning when to listen, when to comfort, when to encourage, and when to be funny. You see, it takes much more than great sex to make a great marriage.

➤ United by God himself

The marriage bond between a man and a woman is created by God himself. God establishes every marriage: whether you marry in a church or a hotel, whether a minister or a Justice of the Peace officiates, whether you love God or loathe him. God created marriage, and he is the one who joins you together.

> 'For this reason a man will leave his father and mother and be united to his wife, and the two will become one flesh.'...Therefore *what God has joined together*, let man not *separate*. Mark 10:7-9 (NIV)

God is personally involved in your marriage. Your marriage is more than just the two of you. It is a three-sided triangle: you, your spouse, and God. God is a party to your marriage whether you intend him to be or not.

In addition, God will hold you accountable. If you are unfaithful, he will deal with you. God will bring adverse circumstances into your life to try to bring you to repentance.

> You ask, "*Why?*" It is because the Lord is acting as the *witness* between you and the wife of your youth, because you have broken faith with her, though she is your partner, the wife of your *marriage* covenant. Malachi 2:14 (NIV)

You see, God takes marriage very seriously, and he wants you to take it seriously, too. When you take your marriage vows, you are making a lifetime commitment. "Till death do us part" is not poetry. It is the reality of your marriage vow.

> A woman is bound to her husband *as long* as he *lives*. But if her husband dies, she is free to marry. 1 Corinthians 7:39 (NIV)

Furthermore, you do not get to decide how much you are willing to commit to the marriage. God requires that you commit everything. You don't get to make up your own vows, including certain things and excluding others. God is the one who joins you together, and he sets the terms for your marriage: absolute and total fidelity to your spouse.

> "I *hate* divorce," says the God of Israel…"I hate the *violent dismembering* of the 'one flesh' of marriage." Malachi 2:16 (Mes)

➤ Bonded by sexual intercourse

God has given husbands and wives a very special gift: the physical union of their bodies. In effect, it is God's wedding gift to the couple. Traditionally, sexual intercourse has been viewed as the consummating act of marriage.

> Marriage should be honored by all, and the *marriage bed* kept *pure*, for God will judge the adulterer and all the sexually immoral. Hebrews 13:4 (NIV)

God designed sexual intercourse to bond a man and a woman together irrevocably. The physical union of their bodies is accompanied by the release of hormones that bind them together emotionally.[3] These emotions produce an irrational commitment to each other, a powerful primordial instinct not subject to reason or even to self-interest. In marriage, sexual intercourse powerfully reinforces the commitment that a husband and wife have to one another. It is the ultimate bonding experience for them.

But the very thing that makes sexual intercourse such a good thing within marriage makes it inappropriate and destructive outside of marriage. You see, God says there is no such thing as casual sex. Sexual intercourse changes its partners irrevocably, whether they intend to be emotionally engaged with one another or not.

> And don't you know that if a man *joins* himself to a *prostitute*, he becomes one body with her? For the Scriptures say, "The two are *united* into one." 1 Corinthians 6:16 (NLT)

Sexual intimacy outside marriage is always damaging; it always leaves you with regrets. You see, sexual intercourse was never created to stand alone; it is fulfilling only in the context of marriage. Premarital sex leaves you with memories and images that mock your commitment to your spouse. Moreover, premarital sex develops in you sexual attitudes and habits that are incompatible with the mutuality of marital sex.

Premarital sex is damaging even when you eventually marry your sexual partner. Your decision to marry one another becomes much more difficult because of the irrational emotional tie you have established through sex. It becomes very difficult to sort out whether you have a common purpose in life and whether you desire to move in the same direction.

Moreover, your urgency in making the decision to marry is greatly diminished. As the folk saying says, "Why buy the cow if you're getting the milk for free?" Living together before marriage doesn't hasten your movement toward marriage; in fact, it greatly retards it. And so, you cheat yourselves out of valuable years of marriage, childbearing, and happiness.

Premarital sex always stunts the growth of your relationship. The focus of your relationship invariably becomes sexual, sometimes to the exclusion of everything else. As a result, you fail to develop your friendship, your emotional sensitivity to one another, your intellectual curiosity, your financial compatibility, and your fellowship in the Lord. You even fail to develop affectionate non-sexual touch. Your investment in each other will tend to be selfish rather than unselfish, getting you off to a shakier start in marriage.

Finally, premarital sex deprives you of the self-control you need to be successful in life and in marriage. Success and delayed gratification go hand in hand. Saying no to premarital sex demonstrates your ability to control yourself when confronted by formidable sexual temptation. It is a credible pledge of your lifelong fidelity to your spouse. It lays a foundation of trust for periods of enforced abstinence due to military deployment, business trips, high risk pregnancy, serious illness, and other difficult life circumstances. Conversely, the failure to develop self-control is illustrated by the prevalence of financial problems in marriages where there was premarital sex.

Marriage Exists For a Purpose

Your marriage exists for more than yourselves. God created your marriage to benefit others as well. In fact, much of the fulfillment of marriage comes from meeting the needs of others through your joint efforts.

Marriage serves certain purposes within the larger society. It is an institution with certain codified relationships, rights, and responsibilities. No other institution produces the benefits for others that marriage does, regardless of the money spent. You see, society has a vested interest in the success of your marriage!

➢ Nurturing children

Pregnancy is the natural result of sexual intercourse—the physical dimension of the One Flesh of marriage and God's wedding gift to the couple. Children are a fundamental part of God's plan for marriage.

> *Children* are a *gift* from the Lord; they are a real blessing. Psalm 127:3 (GN)

One of God's purposes in marriage is to provide a protected place—an optimal environment—for children to grow up in. Little wonder, then, that God prohibits sexual intercourse outside of marriage. Marriage provides a protected place for children because of the commitment a husband and wife have to love one another. Marriage provides an optimal environment for children because the presence of both male and female brings balance and wisdom to the home.

> Didn't the Lord make you *one* with your wife? In body and spirit you are his. And what does he want? *Godly children* from your union. Malachi 2:15 (NLT)

Today with the advent of birth control, children are an afterthought in many marriages. Indeed, one of the reasons for the startling rise in infertility is that children have become an afterthought in so many marriages. As a result, couples delay having children until the most fertile years of childbearing have passed. But children are not an afterthought to God. They are part of his central plan.

> God said to them, "Be *fruitful* and *multiply*, and fill the earth, and subdue it." Genesis 1:28 (NAS)

Therefore, before you marry, you and your beloved need to be very clear about your plans for children. You need to be of one mind about whether you plan to have children, how large a family you wish to have, and how long you wish to wait before becoming pregnant. These decisions cannot be deferred; they are part of discerning your common calling. If you ignore these questions until after you are married, you invite heartbreak for one or both of you.

Also, if either of you have children from a prior marriage, these children are part of God's plan for your new marriage. Meeting their needs must be more important to you than having your own needs met. As a step-parent, you must be able to embrace your step-child as your own child. This is true regardless of the child's custody arrangements, because if you try to ignore his/her existence, you are creating an irreconcilable conflict with your spouse.

> ## ➤ Creating wealth

> Build *homes*, and plan to stay. Plant *gardens*, and eat the food you produce. Marry and have children…And work for the peace and *prosperity* of Babylon. Jeremiah 29:5-7 (NLT)

Marriage is the fundamental economic unit of society. When husband and wife establish a home, they create a very efficient means of meeting the needs of themselves, their children, the aged, and the infirm. You have only to consider the cost of various social programs to understand how efficiently a functioning family meets the needs of its members.

In order to provide for themselves and others, a couple must work hard, they must be industrious, and they must create wealth—building houses and planting gardens, so to speak. Also, because they are invested in the future through their children, they are willing to make sacrifices for long term goals. Their behavior brings prosperity to themselves and to the community in which they live.

> Fill the earth with people and bring it under your *control. Rule over* the fish in the ocean, the birds in the sky, and every animal on the earth. Genesis 1:28 (CEV)

William Galston has pointed out that you need only do three things to avoid poverty in this country: finish high school, marry before having a child, and produce the child after age 20. Those who follow this advice have only an 8% poverty rate, but 79% of those who don't live in poverty.[4] Moreover, single mothers are nine times more likely to live in deep poverty than the married family.[5] Their children are twice as likely to drop out of high school.[6]

You see, families are powerful economic engines in society. It is not religious drivel to say that the health of a society depends upon strong families; it is hard economic fact.[7] Our federal and state governments have recognized the economic value of marriage to society by granting favorable tax treatment to families and by providing certain legal protections to marriage.

Now if you are the non-custodial parent of a minor child, you are probably obligated for child support. Your new spouse must be able to embrace this financial obligation without resentment, out of love for your child. Now is the time to count this cost, not later. You see, it is very important that you show faithfulness and generosity in making these payments. And you should prayerfully consider helping the child through college, even though your legal obligation will end at age 18.

> But if anyone does not *provide* for his own, and especially for those of his *household*, he has *denied* the faith and is worse than an unbeliever. 1 Timothy 5:8 (NAS)

➤ Providing moral training

One of the great responsibilities of marriage is training the next generation. Children need to be taught certain behaviors and attitudes in order for them to succeed in adulthood, and much of what they need to know doesn't come naturally to them. The lessons must be repeated over and over again until they are internalized by the child.

Errant behaviors must be corrected so that the child can learn what is right, and defiance must be punished so that the child can learn self-control. As surely as arrows need to be aimed at their target, your children will need to be directed along the right path.

> Children born to a young man are like sharp *arrows* in a warrior's *hands*. How happy is the man whose quiver is *full* of them! Psalm 127:4-5 (NLT)

You see, much of the training a child needs to be successful in life is moral training. It is learning behaviors and attitudes (not facts), and it takes a tremendous amount of repetition and practice. That is why no social institution can train a child as effectively as his/her parents can.

> Teach them to your children, and *talk* about them when you sit at *home* and walk along the *road*, when you *lie down* and when you *get up*. Deuteronomy 6:7 (NCV)

Parents with intact marriages have a huge advantage in training their children. Divorced parents are much less likely to deliver a united message or to be consistent in their handling of a child. Society loses when a child's parents are divorced.

There are tremendous social and economic consequences when parents fail in the moral training of their children. For example, Al Sanders compared the descendents of two eighteenth century Massachusetts contemporaries: Max Jukes and Jonathan Edwards.[8] Mr. Jukes was an atheist who lived a godless life. His progeny included 310 paupers, 150 criminals, 7 murderers, 100 drunkards, and 130 prostitutes, who cost the state $1.25 million. In contrast, Jonathan Edwards was a great American preacher-evangelist. His progeny included 100 preachers and missionaries, 13 college presidents, 65 professors, 60 authors, 30 judges, 100 lawyers, 60 physicians, 75 military officers, 80 public servants, 3 senators, and 1 vice-president of the United States—who did not cost the state a penny.

The moral training that children receive from their parents prepares them for educational success. Noted black anthropologist John Ogbu found that affluent black parents in Shaker Heights were failing to pass on their work ethic to their children, resulting in a significant achievement gap between black and white students of similar socioeconomic advantages.[9] Abigail and Stephan Thernstrom found that children of any racial group or socioeconomic background could achieve outstanding academic scores provided they followed the pattern of high academic achievers: behaving themselves in class, spending more time in study and homework and less time watching TV, and having parents who did not tolerate low grades (or even medium grades).[10] The Thernstroms concluded that the learning gap between Asian, white, black, and Hispanic students was primarily attributable to the academic expectations and standards that parents in different cultural groups established for their children.[11]

➤ Meeting spiritual needs

> God made husbands and wives to become one body and *one spirit* for his *purpose*. Malachi 2:15 (NCV)

God wants husbands and wives to learn to function together as a spiritual unit. A husband and wife together form the basic spiritual unit of TWO. You see, Jesus promised to release his power whenever two people join together for God's purposes.

> For where *two* or three come together in my name, I am there *with them*. Matthew 18:20 (GN)

This means that husbands and wives need to learn to pray together. They need to make it their habit to thank God for his blessings and to thank him for answered prayers. They need to learn to bring all their needs to God, to seek him for direction in their lives, and to listen and wait for his provision.

Dennis Rainey, Executive Director of FamilyLife, has discovered that couples who pray together regularly (only about 8% of all couples) have the highest levels of marital satisfaction.[12] You see, prayer with God is an intimate form of communication that demands complete honesty and humility. Therefore, the very process of praying together knits your hearts together. Moreover, receiving answers to your prayers and direction for your lives strengthens your unity, builds your faith, and gives you a common purpose.

Finally, husbands and wives should think of themselves as a ministry team. You see, God wants you to move beyond being consumers of his encouragement and blessings. He wants you to learn to give yourselves in service to others. Husbands and wives are uniquely equipped to serve together as a ministry team: in their family, in their church, and in their larger community.

> ...to prepare God's *people* for works of *service*, so that the body of Christ may be *built up*. Ephesians 4:12 (NIV)

➤ Experiencing God's heart

At times, God uses the metaphor of a groom with his bride to try to describe his motives and his heart toward you.

> And as the *bridegroom* rejoices over the bride, so your God will *rejoice* over you. Isaiah 62:5 (NAS)

> "A man leaves his father and mother and is joined to his wife, and the two are united into one." This is a great mystery, but it is an *illustration* of the way *Christ* and the *church* are one. Ephesians 5:31-32 (NLT)

Living together as husband and wife will give you first hand experience of this metaphor. In other words, you will begin to understand more completely how God thinks about you as you think about your spouse. You will understand how powerful God's love for you is as you experience your love for your spouse. You will understand God's forgiveness and forbearance toward you as you reach out to your spouse when he/she has blown it. Your experiences with your spouse will give you insight into God's heart toward you. As a result, you will be better able to see others as God sees them and love them as he loves them.

God also uses the metaphors of a father and a mother with their children to try to describe his heart toward you.

> You saw how the Lord your God *carried* you, as a *father* carries his son. Deuteronomy 1:31 (NIV)

> I will *comfort* you as a *mother* comforts her child. Isaiah 66:13 (NCV)

Having children of your own will give you first hand experience of these metaphors. As you experience the fierceness of your love for your child, your patience with your child's developmental immaturity, your joy in the little victories of childhood, your delight in your child's smiles and hugs and words, your instinctive protectiveness toward your child, your hopes and dreams for what your child can become, and your tender desire to nurture your child, you will gain insight into God's love for you. Loving your child helps you to understand God's heart toward you and to grow in your own love for others.

➢ Overcoming selfishness

One of the great things about marriage is that it helps you overcome your innate selfishness. In marriage, you will have many ready-made opportunities to grow your character and improve your behavior.

Living in close physical proximity with someone will test you in ways that you could never be tested living alone. Being in an emotionally intimate relationship with someone will reveal character flaws that had previously remained hidden. Being responsible for a tiny, helpless baby whose needs are constant and unrelenting will provide you with the opportunity to take your selflessness to a whole new level.

> Whenever trouble comes your way, let it be an *opportunity* for joy. For when your faith is *tested,* your endurance has a chance to *grow.* So let it grow, for when your endurance is fully developed, you will be strong in character and ready for anything. James 1:2-4 (NLT)

Being tested in the area of selfishness is a good thing, because you will be much happier and your relationships will be more satisfying as you learn to put your selfishness behind you. You see, instead of making you happy, selfishness eventually and inevitably makes you sad.

In addition, the responsibilities that come with marriage and children help you to develop effective leadership, better manage your resources, increase your coping skills, and multi-task with aplomb. Your family is a great training ground for future responsibilities.

> If a man does not know how to *manage* his own *household*, how will he take care of the *church* of God? 1 Timothy 3:5 (NAS)

Husbands and Wives Have Different Roles

Because God created men and women to reflect different aspects of his character, his motives, his strength, and his creativity, God has given husbands and wives different functions in their marriage. Understanding and embracing these God-given roles is absolutely essential to the success of your marriage and the satisfaction you will derive from it. Remember, neither of you has been given the complete package. You must learn to depend upon each other, letting your strengths complement and balance each other.

➢ Husbands lead their families

God has called men to be the leaders of their homes. That's what being the head of something means, whether it's your family, a Boy Scout troop, or a Fortune 500 company. You need to set the course, and you are responsible for the outcome. The buck stops with you. God holds you as a husband accountable for the well-being of your family.

> The *husband* is the *head* of the wife as Christ is the head of the church. Ephesians 5:23 (NIV)

It is not enough for you as a husband to kick back and passively enjoy your marriage. You have a responsibility to seek God's direction for your family, to actively engage with your wife and children, to continually be on the lookout for their well-being, and to lead by setting the example for your family. When husbands become dissatisfied with their marriages, it is often because they have stopped leading and have become passive and disengaged.

> Husbands, *love* your wives…cleansing her by the washing with water through the *word*. Ephesians 5:25-26 (NIV)

You as a husband need to provide spiritual leadership for your family. You need to set the example in prayer and Bible study and church attendance, not be dragged along by your wife. You need to cultivate your personal relationship with God as well as a spiritual relationship with your wife.

When God gave the instructions about what fruit in the Garden of Eden could and could not be eaten, he gave those instructions to Adam. Eve was not yet even created! You see, husbands are responsible for charting the course and setting the moral boundaries for their families. That's what it means to lead, and God holds you, the husband, personally accountable for your leadership—or lack thereof.

> And the LORD God *commanded* the man, "You are free to eat from any tree in the garden; but you *must not eat* from the tree of the knowledge of good and evil, for when you eat of it you will surely die." Genesis 2:16-17 (NIV)

God has equipped you as a husband to be able to lead your family. Scientists have recently discovered that male brains seem to be hard-wired for **systematic thought**, having more white matter than female brains.[13] As a result, men are generally good at spatial reasoning and at inductive reasoning (at moving from specific details to broader generalizations and theories). Also, they are able to sustain a single-minded, emotionally detached focus on tasks. You see, God equipped you to be good at seeing the "big picture" so that you can make good decisions and effectively lead your family.

In contrast, God has given women abilities in areas where men are weak. Recent scientific research has shown that female brains seem to be hard-wired for **empathetic thought**. Women's brains have more gray matter and are more densely packed with neurons and dendrites. Furthermore, the white matter in their brains is concentrated in the part of the brain that links the two hemispheres.[14]

As a result, women enjoy an advantage on all language tasks. Also, they are much better at reading the feelings of others, inferring their intentions, picking up contextual clues, and seeing alternate sides of an argument. While husbands may be good at making the final decision, they desperately need the input of their wives in order to make a good decision.

> Husbands, in the same way be *considerate* as you live with your wives, and treat them with *respect* as the weaker partner and as *heirs* with you of the gracious gift of life, so that nothing will hinder your prayers. 1 Peter 3:7 (NIV)

Husbands and wives need each other to be successful. They need to listen to each other with respect, and they need to respect the insights that each has to offer. In fact, a husband who is domineering will most likely be a failure. Furthermore, as the leader in the home, he has a greater obligation to serve his wife than she does to serve him!

> No one ever *hated* his own body, but he feeds and *cares* for it, just as Christ does the church...Each one of you also must *love* his wife as he loves himself. Ephesians 5:29-33 (NIV)

➢ Wives follow their husband's leadership

A wise wife respects the leadership of her husband because she appreciates the different strengths that they bring to marriage. Submit simply means that she is following his leadership, that she is not fighting him for control, and that she is not struggling to have the final say.

> Wives, *submit* to your husbands as to the Lord...and the wife must *respect* her husband. Ephesians 5:22,33 (NIV)

You see, nobody is in control all of the time. Everybody has somebody they report to. Line workers report to supervisors. Teachers report to principals. School superintendents report to school boards. Children report to parents. Soldiers report to commanding officers. CEOs report to boards of directors. Even Jesus reported to the Father.

> I came *from* God and now I am here. I did not come on *my own authority*, but he sent me. John 8:42 (GN)

Every effective organization has an organizational chart, whether it is written down or not. An org chart is simply a map of relationships within the organization. It shows who reports to whom and who is responsible for what. Moreover, authority exists not only at the top, but is distributed throughout the organization—ideally with each person having responsibilities commensurate with their interests and abilities.

God's org chart for marriage specifies that the wife reports to the husband. However, the husband is not a law unto himself, because he reports to God. You see, God—not the husband—is at the top of marriage's org chart! In current business vernacular, you might think of the wife as the family's COO (chief operating officer), the husband as the family's CEO (chief executive officer), and God as the Board of Directors.

Husband and wife both possess roles that are challenging and fulfilling. Each has a broad authority to act for the good of the family and an astounding range of responsibilities. Neither role is more important than the other. Moreover, your husband is responsible to God not only for the direction he sets for your family, but also for how well he listens to you and for how well he nurtures and utilizes your gifts and abilities.

Most decision making in your marriage should be by consensus. However, in the rare instances in which you cannot agree and the decision cannot be deferred, the decision belongs to your husband. As his wife, you have got to let go and give up control. You must learn to trust your husband to make the right decision for your family. Trust that he sees something you don't.

> That is the way the holy women of old made themselves *beautiful*. They *trusted* God and accepted the *authority* of their husbands. 1 Peter 3:5 (NLT)

Even if you disagree with your husband's decision, you can respect and follow his leadership, because your ultimate trust is in God, not in your husband or his decision. You can always trust God to work through the situation, to take care of your family's immediate needs, and to accomplish good things in the long term.

Once you have shared your reservations about a decision with your husband, you should do everything in your power to make his choice successful. Even if the decision turns out to be a bad one, never let the words, "I told you so," escape your lips. Your continued respect for your husband's leadership will allow God to work unhindered in your husband's heart.

> Wives, in the same way be *submissive* to your husbands so that, if any of them do not believe the word, they may be won over *without words* by the behavior of their wives, when they see the purity and *reverence* of your lives. 1 Peter 3:1-2 (NIV)

Finally, the leadership that husbands have in marriage cannot be generalized to the relationship of men and women in general. The Bible does not say that men always lead and women always follow, nor does it say that all women should submit to all men. God's guidelines for marriage are specifically tailored to provide a nurturing environment for children.

Remember that women are not excluded from leadership. Priscilla, the wife of Aquila, is an example of a godly woman who was a gifted teacher and leader in the early church.[15]

➤ Husbands support their families

The sole responsibility for supporting a family financially belongs to the husband. In the creation account, God gave the responsibility for tending the plants in the Garden of Eden to Adam. Again, this was before Eve had even been created.

> The LORD God took the man and put him into the *garden* of Eden to *cultivate* it and keep it. Genesis 2:15 (NAS)

Then when God expelled Adam and Eve from the Garden, he reminded Adam of his responsibility for tending the food supply—in words addressed solely to him. God also warned Adam that because of his disobedience, farming would become a difficult venture, full of risk and setbacks. In the future, the bulk of his time and labor would be spent in providing for his family.

> I have placed a *curse* on the ground. All your life you will *struggle* to scratch a living from it. It will grow thorns and thistles for you, though you will eat of its grains. All your life you will sweat to *produce food*, until your dying day. Genesis 3:17-19 (NLT)

God has equipped men for the physical and emotional demands inherent in supporting their families financially. He has given male bodies greater physical strength, especially the upper body strength needed for manual labor. In his infinite wisdom, God has caused men's primary self-identity to be bound up in the work they do. He has designed men's minds for a single-minded, emotionally detached focus on tasks, thereby enabling them to distance themselves from financial worry and uncertainty.

Therefore, a husband must not require his wife to "carry her own weight" financially. Supporting the family is his responsibility, not hers. Most troubling today is the situation in which a young mother wants to stay home with her baby, but the husband is unwilling for her to quit her job. In this situation the husband needs to do a "gut check." If he is afraid to be the sole support of his family, he is failing to trust God to provide for his family. If he is unwilling to accept a lower standard of living for the well-being of his family, he is valuing a consumer lifestyle over relationships, his priorities are out of kilter, and he is missing out on what God says is the most important thing.

However, wives are not prohibited from seeking paid employment. In fact, the Virtuous Woman in Proverbs 31 appears to have had two separate businesses.

In the first, she wove cloth from wool and linen,[16] made robes and sashes from the cloth, and sold them to merchants.[17] She used her earnings from this first business[18] to buy land and establish a vineyard.[19] She even seems to have had several employees whose work she directed.[20]

➤ Wives make children their priority

When God expelled Adam and Eve from the Garden, the words he directed to Eve concerned children (as yet unborn). You see, God wanted Eve to make her children her primary focus, her priority. By choosing the words he did, God was saying that nothing Eve could do was more important to him than caring for her children. But he also warned her that nurturing her children would be difficult—both physically and emotionally.

> I will greatly increase your *pains*[21] in childbearing; with *pain*[22] you will give birth to *children*.[23] Your desire will be for your *husband,* and he will rule over you. Genesis 3:16 (NIV)

This verse contains two different words for pain. The first refers to *physical* pain and toil, while the second refers to *emotional* pain and sorrow. Nurturing children—meeting their physical, intellectual, and emotional needs and training them in moral behavior and spiritual devotion—is hard work. It takes everything you have to give, and then some. It will require your every waking hour and constant vigilance.

Children don't raise themselves. Nurturing and training a child requires a significant expenditure of effort. Nor can children be viewed as lifestyle accessories, like a house in the suburbs or a club membership. Children are precious to God, and you are accountable to him for them! For that reason, you should be hesitant to delegate the responsibility of caring for your children to others.

Although this verse refers explicitly to pregnancy and childbirth, the word for children does not refer to infants or young children. Interestingly, the Hebrew word *Ben* that is used refers to sons in the broadest sense, including the concepts of grandson, subject, and nation.

Children are a long-term commitment. They are more than just diapers and nursery rhymes. It takes endurance and perseverance to train a child, to mentor an adolescent, and to nurture a young adult. In fact, children always need much more of your time than you anticipate, and they will continue to need you long after you think they should. Remember, though, that while your commitment will be ongoing, so will your influence for good.

However, God placed Eve's responsibility for her children within the context of her marriage, her ongoing desire for her husband, and his leadership of the family. Children need and deserve to grow up in a stable family, where the parents are tightly bonded together, and the father protects and leads the entire family. Especially in the early years of infancy and toddlerhood, the most important way a man can nurture his children is to nurture their mother.

> He settles the barren woman in her *home* as a happy *mother* of children. Psalm 113:9 (NIV)

Although nurturing children is demanding work, it is also deeply satisfying, bringing joy and contentment into a mother's life.

God has uniquely equipped women to nurture their children. He designed female bodies for pregnancy and breastfeeding. He hard-wired female brains for picking up contextual clues, for reading emotional states, and for language fluency so that a woman can be responsive to her child's needs. At the appointed time, God awakens within each woman the deep-seated desire to nurture little ones by means of her "biological clock."

➢ Babies need their mothers

Babies have a bond with their mothers that begins in the womb. During the last trimester of pregnancy we know that babies recognize their mothers' voices. Scientists have documented that a baby's heartbeat declines and then returns to normal at the sound of his mother's voice.[24]

Before the advent of bottles and formula, all babies were breast-fed. Even today, the American Academy of Pediatrics recommends breastfeeding as the optimal form of infant nutrition. Human breast milk contains immune factors and reduces the incidence of many diseases.[25] It also contains the fatty acids DHA and AA which have been shown to improve an infant's memory, language development, and problem solving.[26]

> Can a mother *forget* the baby at her *breast* and have no compassion on the child she has borne? Isaiah 49:15 (NIV)

God has built into breastfeeding a social interaction between mother and child that meets all of the child's sensory, emotional, social, intellectual, and spiritual needs. Understanding this dynamic can help you understand your child's need for YOU (whether or not you choose to breastfeed).

Breast milk is easily digested, and so nursing infants need to be fed between eight and twelve times daily (about every two to three hours).[27] The frequent feedings mean breast-fed infants receive lots of holding and skin-to-skin contact as a matter of course. Interestingly, researchers have found that high levels of touch increase the neural connections in infants' brains and their scores on cognitive tests.[28] Moreover, premature infants receiving forty-five minutes of massage daily had better sleep, increased alertness, longer attention spans, greater responsiveness to their parents, and positive changes in their immune systems.[29]

> Like babies you will be *nursed* and *held* in my arms and bounced on my knees. Isaiah 66:12 (NCV)

A nursing infant is able to regulate his mother's milk supply if he is allowed to nurse on demand.[30] More frequent nursing increases the milk supply while less frequent nursing reduces it, giving the nursing mother a built-in incentive to respond to her baby's cries. Interestingly, researchers have found that infants learn trust (and cry less) when their cries are responded to promptly.[31] You see, your baby develops trust when you respond to his cries: trust that his needs will be met, that he is loved and cared for, and that he can be successful. By being attentive to your baby's needs, you teach him to trust God. Wow.

> Yet you brought me out of the womb; you made me *trust* in you even at my mother's *breast*. Psalm 22:9 (NIV)

Researchers have found that responsiveness to children's needs teaches them empathy,[32] facilitates their moral development,[33] and stimulates critical thinking and higher order learning.[34] Not surprisingly, kindergarteners who had strong attachments to their mothers were judged by their teachers and their peers to be more likeable, more confident, and more successful.[35]

At about six months of age, babies develop a decided preference for their own mothers.[36] At that age, a baby will protest separation from his mother by crying. In fact, even when a mother is abusive, her baby will desperately try to cling to her.[37] You see, you are not a replaceable cog to your baby! You are his whole world. You are his security.

> As a mother *comforts* her *child*, so will I comfort you. Isaiah 66:13 (NIV)

However, if a baby endures repeated or prolonged separation from his mother, he begins to despair and withdraws into himself.[38] However, because their babies stop crying at separation, many parents wrongly assume that everything is OK. Unfortunately the baby's attachment to his mother is at risk, and he may eventually become indifferent to her affection.[39] In fact, researchers have found that the more hours a young child spends away from his mother, the more "disengaged" he is from her when they are together.[40]

The quality of your emotional relationship to your baby matters, and it matters in some unexpected ways. His emotional connection with you stimulates his intellectual development—it is what makes him want to learn about the world.[41] Your emotionally expressive face, especially your eyes, are the most important visual stimulus in your infant's environment. When your infant returns your gaze, endorphin levels rise in both you and your child.[42]

Your attentiveness to your baby, your emotional sensitivity to his desire for stimulation and play, followed by your sensitivity to his need to withdraw and rest, provide the alternate cycles of central nervous system stimulation and cerebral circuit pruning necessary for optimal brain development.[43]

Moreover, the shaming episodes in which mothers correct the behavior of their toddlers (the ubiquitous NO! that in some studies was uttered approximately every nine minutes) have been found to stimulate the brain's right hemisphere and to develop a child's creativity, emotion, and sensitivity—provided that the shaming period is short, and the child makes a quick emotional recovery with the mother.[44]

> We were *gentle* among you, like a mother *caring* for her little children. 1 Thessalonians 2:7 (NIV)

Researchers have found that babies develop language by being spoken to in one-on-one conversations with someone who engages them emotionally and who is able to sensitively decode their verbalizations. Indeed, they have found that no one does these tasks better than the baby's own mother.[45]

In the same way that breastfeeding is the optimal form of infant nutrition, the care of babies by their own mothers is the optimal form of child care, and all other arrangements are evaluated by how closely they achieve the same results. Researchers have found that young children (under 3 years) experienced increased levels of cortisol (a stress hormone) during their afternoons in day care—but not on the days they were at home.[46] In addition, a national long-term study has found that the more hours children spend in child care, the higher the incidence of problem behavior (such as difficulty getting along with others, over-assertiveness, aggressiveness, and disobedience) and the greater its severity.[47] Not coincidentally, other researchers have found that the more time a mother spends apart from her child, the less responsive and "attuned" she is to her baby's needs.[48]

Children do not benefit at all from peer group settings until they are three years old, and then only for short periods of time.[49] In fact, the best way for your baby to learn about the world is to be taken along on your errands while you talk to him about what you are seeing and experiencing.[50] You see, God has equipped you to provide everything your baby needs.

Homework
Lesson #4: The Nature of Marriage

God Created Marriage

1. Which statement in this section was the most helpful to you? Why?

2. Which of the scripture verses quoted in this section is your favorite? Why?

3. Which area of your multifaceted relationship with your beloved is most under-developed?

4. In what area do you and your beloved most need to develop self-control?

Marriage Exists For a Purpose

5. Which statement in this section was the most helpful to you? Why?

6. Which of the scripture verses quoted in this section is your favorite? Why?

7. Do you plan to have children? How many and how soon?

8. If applicable: What are your feelings toward your future step-children?

9. What can you do to make prayer an integral part of your relationship?

Husbands and Wives Have Different Roles

10. Which statement in this section was the most helpful to you? Why?

11. Which of the scripture verses quoted in this section is your favorite? Why?

12. Do you believe that the husband is the leader of his family? Why?

13. Is the male in your relationship a natural leader?

14. Does the female in your relationship like to be in control?

15. How do you understand the wife's role in marriage?

16. Do you plan on being a two paycheck family?

17. Do you want your children to have a stay-at-home mom?

18. How can you prepare financially for a one paycheck future?

Lesson #5: Becoming One

The goal of marriage is unity with your spouse. The Bible describes it as Two Becoming One.

> "For this reason a man will leave his father and mother and be united to his wife, and the *two will become one* flesh." So they are no longer two, but one. Mark 10:7-8 (NIV)

Being Equally Yoked

Your first task in becoming one is to pick the right spouse. How can you know that your beloved is the one for you? How can you know that you're not making a mistake? For some, these questions can be daunting. In fact, few individuals enter into marriage without occasional misgivings.

Popular culture frames the issue something like this, "How can I know that I'm really in love with this person? How can I know that our love will last?" But if you've been paying attention thus far, you know that these aren't the right questions to ask. Sexual chemistry and human love aren't enough for a lasting marriage.

The Bible frames the issue in another way. The oneness of marriage is not some mystical, emotional union of your true selves. Marriage is much more all-encompassing than your emotions—it is a union of your lives.

> Be ye not *unequally yoked* together with unbelievers. 2 Corinthians 6:14 (KJV)

The Bible says that when you marry someone, it's like getting into a yoke with them. The metaphor of the yoke refers to the piece of wood that joins two animals so that they can pull together effectively. But unless the two animals placed in the yoke are well-suited to one another, they will end up pulling against each other instead.

> You shall not plow with an *ox* and a *donkey* together. Deuteronomy 22:10 (NAS)

And so the questions you need to ask yourself as you approach marriage are these: Are you equally yoked? Do you make a good team? Can you fit comfortably in a yoke with your beloved? Will you be pulling in the same direction? Are you well-suited to one another?

➢ Common faith

Your relationship to God is the foundation of your life. It influences everything about you: what you think, how you act, and what your goals are. Therefore, it is absolutely essential that you and your spouse be of the same faith.

Christ followers should only marry those who follow Christ. They must not marry "unbelievers," that is, those who do not share their faith. This includes individuals who practice another faith—such as Jews, Mormons, Muslims, Hindus, New Agers—as well as atheists (people who deny God exists) and agnostics (people who don't think it matters whether God exists or not).

> Do not be bound together with unbelievers; for what *partnership* have righteousness and lawlessness, or what fellowship has *light* with *darkness*? Or what harmony has Christ with (the Devil), or what has a believer in common with an unbeliever? 2 Corinthians 6:14-15 (NAS)

You see, different faiths cannot be mixed together. They are incompatible with one another. Trying to observe two faiths, or trying to honor both traditions by celebrating two sets of religious holidays, is in fact to deny the truth of either one.

A Christian who marries an unbeliever will almost inevitably drift away from God. You may stop practicing your faith in order to avoid conflict with your spouse. Or you may embrace your spouse's religious observances. In either case, you will have forsaken the Lord.

> Do not marry any of them, and do not let your children marry any of them, because then they would *lead* your children *away* from the Lord to worship *other gods*. Deuteronomy 7:3-4 (GN)

Moreover, being a Christian is much more than having the correct belief system or practicing certain behaviors. When you become a Christian, God himself comes to live in you, and he transforms you from the inside out.

> For we are the *temple* of the living God. As God said: "I will *live in them* and walk among them. I will be their God, and they will be my people. 2 Corinthians 6:16b (NLT)

Because God himself dwells in you, you must not marry an unbeliever. If you do, the Spirit of God in you will be at war with the ungodly spirit in your spouse.

> How can *Christ* and the *Devil* agree? What does a believer have in common with an unbeliever? How can God's *temple* come to terms with pagan idols? 2 Corinthians 6:15-16a (GN)

You were made to know God, to have a relationship with God, to fellowship with him, and to receive comfort, direction, and empowerment from him. Wow. Your deepest fellowship with others will always come in God's presence, because God touches us at a level that is profound, that is beyond words, and that is life-changing.

When a husband and wife jointly follow Christ, it brings unity to their marriage in many ways and on many levels. Simply put, following Christ puts you in sync with one another, giving you love for each other and a common direction.

> …give you a spirit of *unity* among yourselves as you *follow Christ* Jesus. Romans 15:5 (NIV)

Indeed, spouses need to be compatible in their desire to follow Christ. In other words, one cannot be "hot" and the other "cold." God cannot be very important to one of you and of marginal importance to the other. Your passion for knowing God, for obeying him, and for serving him needs to be similar and complementary. Your desire to grow spiritually, to be changed by him, and to step out in faith should be roughly equivalent.

Spouses also need to be compatible in their understanding of how to follow Christ. You need to be similar in the length of time that you have walked with the Lord, to be roughly equivalent in your "newness" or your "seasoning" in following Christ. You need a common understanding about how God speaks to you and how he leads and guides you. You need to be in agreement about the behaviors God requires and prohibits. And you need to find a church home that meets the emotional and spiritual needs of you both.

> ➢ **Compatible personal values**

There are many decisions in life that are largely a matter of personal preference. There is almost always more than one way to follow a Biblical guideline, and the way you choose will reflect your personality, your abilities, your current situation, and your understanding of the life God has called you to. Each of you has a system of personal preferences and values that helps to define you and to guide your life.

In order to achieve unity, husbands and wives need to have compatible personal preferences and values. That is, they need to be like-minded.

> If you have any encouragement from being *united* with Christ...then make my joy complete by being *like-minded*. Philippians 2:1-2 (NIV)

The following questions can help you identify your personal preferences and values. Do you like to be physically active, and/or do you enjoy being outdoors? How sociable are you, and how important are your friends or your family to you? Do you need down time or personal space?

What do you do to relax? What sort of events do you like to attend (sports, movies, museums)? Do you have a hobby, and how expensive is it? Are you interested in politics? Are you involved in your local community?

How highly do you value education? Did you complete your higher education, and/or do you have educational goals for yourself? What is important to you about your work, and what are your long-term career goals? What material things would you like to acquire, and why?

What does success look like to you? What are your goals for marriage? Where would you like to be in 5 years, in 10 years, in 20 years, in 50 years?

It is important for you to consider whether or not your personal preferences and values are compatible with your beloved's. If they conflict with one another or if they are mutually exclusive, you will have ongoing quarrels, conflict and disappointment. But if you and your spouse are like-minded, you will have peace in your home.

> Finally, brethren, rejoice, be made complete, be comforted, be *like-minded*, live in peace; and the God of love and *peace* will be with you. 2 Corinthians 13:11 (NAS)

➤ Compatible cultural styles

Each of you is a product of the culture you grew up in. You have strong emotional ties to certain foods, certain music, certain clothing, and certain objects that remind you of home and the people in your childhood. That's the whole idea behind "comfort food"—that the food you grew up with comforts you emotionally. It's deeply satisfying to you.

> No one will offer food to *comfort* those who mourn for the dead…nor will anyone give them a drink to *console* them. Jeremiah 16:7 (NIV)

When you marry, you need to be comfortable with the cultural trappings that comfort your spouse. Although they will not have the emotional meaning for you that they do for your beloved, you must feel at home with them. Ideally you should learn to enjoy them. At the very least you must not resent them as intrusions into your married life. Marriage isn't like a trip to Disneyland; you can't leave when you get tired of exciting new cultural experiences.

Moreover, from your upbringing, you will have certain assumptions about how things are done, how men and women should act, how the holidays should be celebrated, how extended families should relate to one another, what makes a place feel (or smell) like home, and how children should behave. You see, we all have expectations about how the world should be ordered, and our expectations are seldom consciously chosen. They are typically the sum of our childhood experiences. All things being equal, the old ways are deeply comforting to us.

> I remember your *ancient laws*, O Lord, and I find *comfort* in them. Psalm 119:52 (NIV)

All couples face cultural adjustments, especially around the holidays. For this reason, it is a good thing to ask yourself how comfortable you feel around your beloved's family and/or extended family, how comfortable you are in their homes, and whether you enjoy their family celebrations. If they embrace you with open arms, are you willing to become an integral part of their family, or do you want to pull your spouse as far away from them as possible? In marriage, your spouse's family is an ongoing part of your life, and you need to be willing to build bridges to them.

If you and your spouse come from significantly different cultures or sub-cultures, you need to consider this issue carefully. You need to count the cost upfront. This is one situation in which love cannot afford to be "blind."

> For which one of you, when he wants to *build* a tower, does not first sit down and *calculate* the *cost* to see if he has enough to complete it? Luke 14:28 (NAS)

You need to ask yourself if you are comfortable in your beloved's culture and whether you are willing to identify yourself with his/her people. Or, do their ways seem alien and uncomfortable to you? Do you want to hold yourself apart from your beloved's culture? Do you feel like an "outsider" emotionally?

➤ Common purpose

God wants your marriage to be a testimony to the world. He wants your marriage to be a powerful example of his goodness and the rightness of his ways. In a world of brokenness, God wants you to reach out to others and share his love, his healing, and his redemptive power.

> May God who gives endurance and encouragement give you a spirit of *unity* among yourselves as you *follow* Christ Jesus, so that with one heart and mouth you may *glorify* the God and Father of our Lord Jesus Christ. Romans 15:5-6 (NIV)

In the same way that God has a unique plan for each individual, he has a unique plan for each marriage—a calling, if you will. You see, each married couple has a unique contribution to make to the world and within the church. No one else can make the contribution that you can make because no one else has the same mix of personality, experience, interests, and abilities that you possess.

> Under (Christ's) direction, the whole body is *fitted together* perfectly. As each part does its *own special work*, it helps the other parts grow, so that the whole body is healthy and growing and full of love. Ephesians 4:16 (NLT)

God joins men and women together in marriage so that by working together they can accomplish things that they would be unable to do alone. While he has certain purposes for all marriages, he has specific purposes for your marriage. Therefore, one of the things you need to ask yourselves in considering marriage is, "Do we feel called by God to "do life" together?" It isn't necessary to understand what God's exact purpose is; in fact, that will probably be revealed to you over your entire lifetimes. But you should have a sense that God is bringing you together for a purpose.

> Make my joy complete by being *like-minded*, having the same love, being one in spirit and *purpose*. Philippians 2:2 (NIV)

As you consider marriage, you need to ask yourself what your hopes and dreams and plans for the future are. Then you need to consider whether they are in sync with the hopes and dreams and plans of your beloved. Is God leading you in a common direction?

➤ Consensus about children

> Your wife shall be like a *fruitful vine* within your house, your *children* like olive plants around your table. Psalm 128:3 (NAS)

Throughout the Bible, the birth of children is viewed as a blessing from God. Since children are so central to the purpose of marriage, it is imperative that you and your beloved reach a consensus about children *before* you marry.

First, you need to prayerfully consider what you yourself want. What is your vision of a happy family life? Do you want children? How soon do you want to start a family? How many children do you want to have? What sort of upbringing do you want for them? Who will care for them before they start to school? How do you want them to be educated?

Then you need to discuss these issues with your beloved. Your thoughts at this stage of life may provide only the most general outline for the future. That's OK. What you are looking for is a general consensus between the two of you about the role children will play in your marriage. However, if one of you has strong opinions about any of these issues, it is absolutely essential that the other be in agreement. For example, if one of you wants children and the other doesn't, then you probably shouldn't be considering marriage to each other.

On the other hand, some of you already have children. When that is the case, each of you needs to be able to embrace these children as part of the work God is doing in bringing you two together in marriage. You need to understand that meeting their needs is part of God's plan for your marriage.

> A father to the *fatherless*, a defender of widows…God sets the lonely in *families*. Psalm 68:5-6 (NIV)

If you resent (even a little) the fact that these children exist and will be part of your marriage, then you should not enter into the marriage. All children are precious to God, and their needs are a priority to him. If you are the step-parent, you need to be able to embrace these children as your own, as you rely on God to work in your heart and in your relationship with them. If you are the natural parent, you must learn to relinquish some of the control as you make room for your new spouse in your relationship with your children.

When your beloved is the non-custodial parent, there is the tendency to think that you can just ignore a child's existence. Wrong! That child is a part of your beloved's life, emotions, and responsibilities. Your step-child will influence your family dynamics regardless of the time he/she actually spends in your home. Moreover, this child is precious to God, and God wants you to be an instrument of love in his/her life. Therefore, you must be willing to embrace this child as your own. You must not resent the child support payments as taking something away from you, because when you marry, your beloved's child becomes your responsibility, too.

You see, after you marry, children aren't yours or mine; they are *ours*.

➤ Compatible financial styles

Fighting over money isn't any fun, but many married couples find themselves fighting about money a lot. It doesn't have to be this way. If you and your beloved have compatible financial styles *and* you apply Biblical principles of money management, you will experience unity, not conflict.

Begin by agreeing to apply God's financial principles within your marriage. If your finances are in disarray or if you have never made God a partner in managing your money, you may want to enroll in a course to gain the necessary budgetary tools and Biblical insight. An example of such a course is *Good $ense*, written by Dick Towner of the Willow Creek Association.[1]

Here are some principles to get you started. God needs to be in the center of your financial planning, not an afterthought. One of the best ways to do this is by giving him the *first* part of your income—what the Bible calls firstfruits—not what you have left over at the end of the month, which is typically little or nothing. It is amazing how this simple act of faith can set your priorities in order, bring discipline to your spending, and result in abundant blessings—financial and otherwise.

> *Honor* the Lord with your wealth, with the *firstfruits* of all your crops; then your barns will be filled to *overflowing*, and your vats will brim over with new wine. Proverbs 3:9-10 (NIV)

Most of you know the story of *The Tortoise and the Hare*, in which the slow-moving but persistent turtle beats the fleet-footed but erratic rabbit in a footrace. God blesses the turtles of this world. When you first begin to apply God's principles, it may seem that everyone else is doing better than you are financially, but much of what you are seeing is an illusion. Don't be deceived by the allure of getting rich quick, living large, or keeping up with the Joneses. Over time, you will be amazed at the financial independence you will achieve simply by letting God direct your finances.

> Dishonest money dwindles away, but he who gathers money *little by little* makes it *grow*. Proverbs 13:11 (NIV)

Contentment doesn't depend upon the amount of money or possessions you have. If you are focused on the quantity, you will never have enough. Contentment comes from enjoying what you already have.

> Whoever loves *money* never has money *enough*; whoever loves wealth is never *satisfied* with his income. Ecclesiastes 5:10 (NIV)

You and your beloved need to make a paradigm shift in your thinking, viewing things only as means to an end rather than ends in themselves. Your focus needs to be on living the life God has called you to. Things can be enjoyed. Some things might even be treasured, but acquiring things must never be the focus of your life. If it is, you will miss the things that are truly important.

As you internalize these principles, you should be well on your way to spending less than you earn. In contrast, many in our consumer society typically spend more than they earn, falling behind more and more each month. Spending less than you earn should eliminate most of your money quarrels, all by itself. You see, living within your means is a key to peace in your home, financial freedom, and many spiritual blessings.

These broad guidelines leave lots of room for personal discretion in your spending habits. There is no one right way to spend your money, providing you honor God and live within your means. You may choose to splurge on something that others may scrimp on, and scrimp on things that others find essential. For example, some people buy underwear at Wal-mart, others at Victoria's Secret.

> Don't I have the *right* to do what I want with my own money? Matthew 20:15 (NIV)

You and your beloved need to determine if you have compatible financial styles in spending money. On what things do you like to splurge? On what things do you like to scrimp? Moreover, you need to have similar financial priorities in life. Are you a spender or a saver, and to what extent? What are your financial priorities? Finally, you need to have similar attitudes toward debt and the use of credit cards.

You should have a financial heart-to-heart talk with your beloved. You will become one financially with your spouse in the eyes of the law and bill collectors, and you must not take this step blindly. How much is your beloved's income? How much debt does he/she carry? What kind of debt is it? How much are the payments each month? What assets does he/she own? How much does he/she have in bank accounts, savings, 401(k)s? How does your beloved use credit cards? Is the balance paid in full each month? Are there overdraft fees on his/her bank account? You see, in order to contemplate marriage, you must feel comfortable with both your beloved's financial situation *and* his/her money management style.

➤ Testing your relationship

You need to be able to "be yourself" with your beloved without fear of his/her disapproval. You need to be able to say what you think without fear of rejection. You should not feel that you have to hide any information about yourself or your past in order to be acceptable to him/her. In fact, you should feel exhilarated at being able to be more honest—more transparent—with you beloved than with anyone else in your life. But if you have abandoned any of your beliefs in order to get along with your beloved or if you have stopped doing things that are important to you because he/she doesn't approve, it should be a red flag to you.

Being with your beloved should bring out the best in you, not the worst. You should be a better person because of the influence of your beloved in your life. He/she should believe in you, encourage you, and see things that are worthwhile in you. When your beloved is a positive influence in your life, your friends and family will recognize it and will tend to encourage your relationship. However, if your friends and family are distrustful of your beloved or wary of your involvement with him/her, it should be a red flag to you (unless of course, they have *previously* shown themselves to have a personal agenda other than your happiness).

You should never consider marriage unless your love for the person is greater than your lust for him/her. You see, lust truly makes you blind. Sexual intimacy will cause you to consider a marriage that you would never in your right mind consider otherwise. And so you need to be sexually chaste in order to consider marriage. If you are unwilling to abstain from sex until after you are married, it should be a red flag to you.

God's peace is always the indication that you are proceeding in the right direction with your life. Even though circumstances are hectic around you, perhaps even a little chaotic, you should have an abiding peace in your heart that you are on the right track. Nervousness is to be expected—after all you are making an important commitment that will affect the rest of your life. But if there is a little voice inside you saying, "This isn't right!" it should raise a red flag for you. Likewise, if you and your beloved are fighting with each other as you approach marriage, it should be a red flag to you.

> Let the *peace* of Christ *rule* in your hearts. Colossians 3:15 (NIV)

Finally, don't be afraid that if you want something, God won't let you have it. The Bible says that if you put God in the center of your life, your desires are one of the ways he will direct you. God will change your heart and cause you to desire what he has planned for you, and that includes your beloved and marriage.

> *Delight* yourself in the Lord and he will give you the *desires* of your heart. Psalm 37:4 (NIV)

Leaving and Cleaving

When a couple is married, their relationship to their own parents is fundamentally altered. In marriage you will leave the family unit of your parents and form a new, separate and distinct family unit with your spouse.

> Therefore shall a man *leave* his father and his mother, and shall *cleave* unto his wife: and they shall be *one flesh*. Genesis 2:24 (KJV)

➤ Separate from your parents

When you finished school and began living on your own, your relationship to your parents changed. When you ceased to be financially dependent on them, your responsibilities for yourself increased, and their control over you ended. You see, parents have no right to expect obedience from their adult children. Adult children have an ongoing obligation to honor their parents, but not to obey them.

> *Honor* your *father* and your *mother*, so that you may live long in the land the Lord your God is giving you. Exodus 20:12 (NIV)

Honoring someone means to treat them with respect, to be kind and courteous to them, and to listen with interest to what they have to say. You should value your parents because they gave you life. You should also appreciate the sacrifices they made in raising you. However, honor does not require you to agree with your parents, to take their advice, or to grant every request that they make of you. Honoring your parents does not even require that you like them.

As an unmarried adult, your primary family ties were to your mother and father, and your primary family responsibilities were to them. The holidays, birthdays, and other family celebrations revolved around your parents' home and their family unit.

When you marry, God establishes a new family unit. After you are married, your primary family tie is to your spouse, not to your parents or in-laws. Your primary responsibility is to him/her. Your spouse's needs take priority over the needs of your mother or father. Together you must decide for yourselves how to celebrate the holidays and how to negotiate family gatherings and other obligations. Together you decide what is best for your new family.

This is a daunting transition under the best of circumstances, as both you and your parents seek to establish the boundaries of your new relationship. Expect a certain amount of trial and error to occur, both on your part and on the part of your parents, because there are no hard and fast rules to follow. What a mature relationship between parents and their married children looks like is as unique as the personalities and circumstances involved.

➤ Protect the autonomy of your family unit

Some parents have difficulty accepting the autonomy of their married children. Sometimes this is because the parents simply refuse to accept the new spouse, trying to ignore his/her existence whenever possible, while expecting their adult child to continue to function as their unmarried child with primary ties to them, not the new spouse.

In this situation, you and your spouse will want to be careful to present yourselves to your parents as a single and indivisible decision-making unit. It is entirely appropriate for the child to refuse to visit or interact with the parents unless the spouse accompanies him/her. If the parents try to get the child to agree to something, the response should be, "Let me discuss it with *(spouse's name)*, and I'll get back to you." Your polite but persistent message should be, "This marriage isn't going away, and if you want me, you have to accept my spouse, too."

Other parents gladly embrace the new spouse, but they treat the child and spouse as if they were part of the parents' immediate family, having the same family ties and responsibilities as unmarried children. But when a child marries, he/she leaves the parents' immediate family and becomes part of their extended family instead, because he/she has established his/her own autonomous family unit. Some parents refuse to make this transition in their thinking and behavior toward their married children. Such parents often make heavy demands on the couple's time and intrude upon their privacy.

In this situation, you and your spouse will want to work together to teach the parents that your relationship as a couple takes priority over your participation in their extended family. You should refuse to be manipulated by emotionally needy parents, understanding that the needs of your spouse come before the needs of your parents. You should not feel guilty for encouraging your parents to be more autonomous and to develop friendships of their own instead of relying too heavily upon you. You can teach them that they can be happy and enjoy life without your physical presence at every family gathering, and that your love and care for your new family does not diminish them, but instead reflects well upon them.

Finally, you should realize that it is not your responsibility to make your parents or in-laws happy. If their requests are unreasonable, and if they are unwilling to recognize your obligations to your spouse, they may become very angry with you. However, if you have been respectful toward them, you have done nothing wrong.

> If it is *possible*, as far as it *depends* on you, live at *peace* with everyone. Romans 12:18 (NIV)

You see, it doesn't always depend upon you. If fulfilling your obligations to your spouse and your new family makes your parents unhappy, so be it.

➤ Rely on each other

It is not just your parents who must learn to respect your autonomy as a married couple. As a new husband and wife, you will also be on a learning curve, learning to respect your own autonomy as a family unit and to rely on each other.

You need to learn to respect one another in your new roles as husband and wife. You shouldn't be second-guessing your spouse as he/she seeks to fulfill his/her God-given responsibilities in marriage. You need to learn to trust God to give your spouse strength and wisdom for the benefit of you both. Although it is good to seek the counsel of others, you should value the counsel of your spouse most of all, and learn to rely on it.

Don't betray the trust of your husband or wife. Much that is shared in marriage is intimate and sensitive in nature; don't betray your spouse's vulnerability and transparency with you by gossiping to others.

> An excellent wife, who can find?...The *heart* of her husband *trusts* in her. Proverbs 31:10-11 (NAS)

Furthermore, you should never involve your parents or in-laws in your quarrels. Don't run home to Mama after a fight, and don't ask your parents to choose sides between you. Never complain about your spouse to your parent. It is unfair to the parent, and it dishonors your spouse. If you value a parent's opinion, you may ask for his/her advice in handling a problem, but only if your attitude is respectful toward your spouse.

> *Accept* one another...in order to bring *praise* to God. Romans 15:7 (NIV)

Finally, accept your spouse as the one who is perfectly tailored to your needs and personality. Never unfavorably compare your spouse to your parent or in-law. Don't expect your husband to have all the good qualities your father had; nor can your wife be expected to have all your mother's good qualities, especially when those qualities have been developed over a lifetime. Each of us is unique. Respect and value your spouse's uniqueness.

The Marriage Bed

Sexual intercourse is a powerful bond between husband and wife. God intended it to be so. The union of your bodies is a literal representation of the One Flesh of marriage, but God designed sex to be much more than a physical act. He designed it to encompass your hearts, your minds, your spirits, your vulnerability to one another, and your transparency with one another.

➢ Repentance for past sins

God says that the only pure sexual activity is that between a husband and wife after they are married. And since God created sex, we should trust him that he knows what he is talking about.

Marriage should be *honored* by all, and the marriage bed kept *pure*. Hebrews 13:4 (NIV)

If you have been sexually active at any time with any person (including your beloved) before your marriage, you have dishonored the institution of marriage. You see, you took something that didn't belong to you, but belongs solely to married people. If you continue to excuse that behavior in your own mind, you are continuing to dishonor marriage, even as you make plans for your own wedding. Such an attitude will make it more difficult for you to keep your marriage vow of sexual fidelity.

In addition, if you have been sexually active before marriage, you have defiled yourself. You must bear the burden of sin that keeps you from getting close to God or ever really knowing him. And you must bear the consequences of sin that flow from your short-sided actions. Sexual sin is particularly damaging, because it causes you sin against yourself and against your own body.

In *sexual sin* we violate the sacredness of our *own bodies*, these bodies that were made for God-given and God-modeled love. 1 Corinthians 6:18 (Mes)

Fortunately, God is not surprised by sexual immorality. He long ago made provision for your forgiveness and restoration through Jesus Christ. The only thing that can hold you back is your unwillingness to repent of your past behavior. But if you are willing, God receives your repentance with gladness.

It's not hard to make a clean start with God. Getting over your pride is the hard part. Repentance simply requires you to agree with God that what you did was wrong, to acknowledge your responsibility for the damage your behavior caused, and to resolve that you will act differently in the future with God's help.

Take away my sin, and I will be *clean*. *Wash me*, and I will be whiter than snow. Psalm 51:7 (NCV)

As you allow God to work in your heart and your mind, he will restore you to wholeness and purity. God will change the way you think about things, and he will bring a new joy to your life. If you want to experience the fullness of married sex, it is absolutely essential that you let God purify you from past sins.

➢ Sex is not about your performance

Much of what you have learned from our sex-saturated culture will hinder you in making a healthy sexual adjustment in your marriage. The Sexual Revolution of the 1960's and 70's separated sex from its context of marriage. Without marriage, sex was reduced to a purely physical experience, because true intimacy is possible only within the commitment of marriage.

As a result, our cultural view of sex is performance-based, being framed in terms of who is most skilled at sexual seduction, who has the best sexual endowment, who is having the most frequent sex, who has the longest orgasms, and who experiences the greatest sexual ecstasy. Ironic isn't it that in our sex-saturated culture, advertising for erectile dysfunction prescriptions floods our airwaves? Or that Robert Reich hit a cultural nerve by talking about DINS (dual-income, no-sex couples)?[2]

> You have made my heart *beat faster*, my sister, my bride; You have made my heart beat faster with a single *glance* of your eyes...How beautiful is your love, my sister, my bride! How much better is your love than wine! Song of Solomon 4:9-10 (NAS)

> Awake, north wind! Come, south wind! Blow on my garden and waft its lovely *perfume* to my lover. Let him *come into his garden* and eat its choicest fruits. Song of Solomon 4:16 (NLT)

God designed sexual intercourse to be about relationships, not sexual performance; about making an intimate connection with your spouse, not about your sexual technique. Sexual energy—and its closely related twin, sexual intuition—come from your desire to connect with your spouse, to draw closer to one another, and to know one another in the Biblical sense. True sexual satisfaction comes from enjoying one another, not from meeting any standard set by others.

Sexual relationships are dynamic. Don't expect sexual intercourse to be the same every time, to always hit the same highs, or to always build the same feelings between you. Your body is changeable in its sexual responsiveness. Different things will turn you on at different times. This is particularly true for women, whose responsiveness is affected by menstrual cycles and changes in fertility. If you think of sex as a technique to be mastered or as a pattern to be followed, you will become very frustrated. But if you think of sex as an intimate dialog, you will be exhilarated by your varied experiences. God never intended for sex to become boring or mechanical.

God has designed sexual intercourse so that you must learn from one another. You must learn to communicate your sexual needs to your spouse. It is unreasonable to expect your spouse to read your mind. If you do, you are setting yourself up for sexual frustration. No matter how well your spouse knows you, he/she will always need to know what is working for you at this particular time, which part of your body longs to be touched, and the type of touch that is desired—soothing or exciting, vigorous, teasing, or gentle.

Part of the sexual adjustment of marriage is the development of intimate communication, of verbal and nonverbal cues, and of playful words and leading touch that effectively communicate your sexual needs. Your focus must always be on learning from one another.

In addition, learn some biology. Most couples can benefit from learning about their sexual anatomy—in particular about the female clitoris. Kegel exercises[3] can help women develop muscle tone in the pelvic floor for better sexual responsiveness and easier childbirth. Trusted organizations such as Focus on the Family and FamilyLife have books available on their web sites that address sexual issues frankly and from a Biblical perspective.[4]

➢ Be generous with one another

Lovemaking can be very selfish. It can be all about getting your own needs met and getting the sexual release you desire. The sexual dance can degenerate into a pattern of manipulation—of giving just enough to get what you want. This pattern can occur within marriage, not just outside of it.

When lovemaking becomes selfish, inevitably one of you ends up feeling used, exploited, violated, and unloved. Then the very thing that God designed to draw you closer and bond you ever more tightly together, becomes a point of conflict and frustration in your marriage. God has a better way.

> The *marriage bed* must be a place of *mutuality*—the husband seeking to satisfy his wife, the wife seeking to satisfy her husband. 1 Corinthians 7:3 (Mes)

God wants you to be generous in your lovemaking. He wants you to be at least as concerned about meeting your spouse's sexual needs as you are about your own. You see, the satisfaction of meeting your spouse's needs enriches the experience of you both and adds greatly to your own sexual satisfaction.

Be accommodating toward one another in bed, and be considerate of the other's needs—whether it be for sexual intimacy, for physical comfort or reassurance, or for just plain sleep. Whenever possible, you should accommodate your spouse's desire for sex. However, the marital right for sex does not automatically trump everything else. It must be balanced with your needs and the current circumstances of your married lives. You see, the obligation to be generous with and considerate of one another is mutual.

One of the most generous things you can do for your partner sexually is to help him/her become fully aroused. For men this means an erect and very hard penis; for women this means engorgement of the genital tissues and noticeable vaginal lubrication. Both men and women emit a distinctive musky smell when sexually aroused. Remember, generosity is in your best interest because neither of you will have an optimal sexual experience unless both of you are fully aroused.

Men and women reach sexual arousal by very different routes. Men are aroused by **visual stimuli**—by what they see with their eyes, especially the curving shape of the female body. In contrast, women are aroused by **emotional stimuli**—by their feelings of closeness to their man, of being loved by him, and of having a future with him. Be sure to offer your spouse generous amounts of the stimuli he/she needs most.

Learn to appreciate your differences in sexual responsiveness because they complement one another. The male response to visual stimuli helps keep sexuality on the agenda of your marriage (quantity), while the female response to emotional stimuli helps keep your sexuality focused on the relationship between you (quality).

Men and women also operate on very different sexual timetables. Think of it as the difference between cooking with a microwave and a crockpot. Men's bodies respond quickly; you can be fully aroused within five minutes. In contrast, women's bodies respond slowly; you require approximately twenty to thirty minutes to be fully aroused.

As a couple, you can be frustrated by these differences, or you can learn to make them work for you. You can use the "extra" time to learn to be more transparent with one another, to get to know one another better, to increase your emotional and spiritual closeness, and to enjoy one another more.

Sex should be a private matter just between the two of you. Modesty in this area is very becoming. Never flirt with someone other than your spouse for any reason. Sexual arousal, regardless of what precipitated it, should always be focused back on your spouse alone. In ambiguous social situations, talk about how much you love your husband, your wife, and your kids to let others know of your devotion to your marriage.

➢ **Plan for life-long sex**

> May you rejoice in the wife of your *youth*. A loving doe, a graceful deer—may her breasts *satisfy* you always, may you *ever* be captivated by her love. Proverbs 5:18-19 (NIV)

What is your concept of sexy? Is it Brad Pitt or Julia Roberts? Is it Mel Gibson or Sophia Loren? Typically your concept of sexy is defined for you from media images enhanced by make-up, lighting, film angles, special lenses, cropping, and retouching. Nobody looks like that in real life.

Yet spouses often take those manufactured images of sexiness and expect their own spouses to measure up to them. Husbands get compared to Brad Pitt or Mel Gibson or the hunk down the street. Wives get compared to Julia Roberts or Sophia Loren or the hot chick at the gym. No wonder the romance begins to dissipate. You see, God never intended you to compare yourself or your spouse with others.

> We will not *compare* ourselves with each other as if one of us were *better* and another *worse*…Each of us is an original. Galatians 5:26 (Mes)

If you want to have a sexy marriage, and if you want to still be turned on by your spouse in five years or twenty or fifty, you will focus your attention on the *contrast* between male and female. The intrinsic differences between your body and your spouse's are very sexy, and that sexiness will persist throughout life's changes and bumps—pregnancy, aging, and illness. If you nurture your appreciation of these differences, you will continue to delight in each other.

How can you keep the romance alive? The notion of romance is something of a black hole to many men, who resent having to buy flowers and cards, and who are frustrated by their wives' requests to "be more romantic." But the heart of romance is demonstrating your love through acts of kindness. Romance is expressing your love in tangible, symbolic ways. You see, it's not the flowers themselves that are romantic; it's the love that seeks to express itself by bringing the flowers that is romantic. Nor is any song particularly romantic, it's the song's ability to bring to mind your shared experiences that makes it romantic.

You see, romance isn't so much about what you do, but about the motive behind your actions. In fact, many women find it very sexy when their husbands do housework. It's not the housework itself that is sexy. It's the love that performs an undesirable task so that she doesn't have to that produces her emotional response to him.

> Greet one another with a *holy* kiss. 2 Corinthians 13:12 (NAS)

Non-sexual physical affection is very important to the health of your marriage. Hugging, holding hands, and walking arm in arm are important ways of communicating your encouragement, contentment, affection, and solidarity to one another. Part of the sexual adjustment in marriage is to learn when sexual touch is appropriate and when it is not. You see, every marriage needs a well-developed vocabulary of affectionate, non-sexual touch in order to express the multifaceted nature of your relationship.

Too many husbands make every touch a sexual touch. The unintended result is to reduce physical contact and intimacy with their wives, not increase it. If every touch is a sexual invitation, the emotional and spiritual needs of your wife will go unmet. Don't be surprised then, if she starts resenting and avoiding you.

Finally, we live in a sex-saturated culture that presents sex as THE most important thing in your lives. The reality is different. Sex is estimated to contribute only fifteen to twenty percent to a couple's satisfaction in marriage.[5] It's not the most important thing, even in your marriage.

Moreover, sex will be more important at some times in your marriage than at others. Your interest in sex may ebb and flow, like the waves of the ocean. Sometimes it will be high tide, but sometimes it will be low tide. The presence of pre-teens and teenagers in the home can be hard on the sex lives of their parents. Pregnancy and illness can be, too. Accept it as part of your life together and focus on building your closeness in other ways.

Homework
Lesson #5: Becoming One

Being Equally Yoked

1. Which statement in this section was the most helpful to you? Why?

2. Which of the scripture verses quoted in this section is your favorite? Why?

3. How are you alike in your faith? How are you different?

4. How are you alike in your personal preferences? How are you different?

5. How were your cultural backgrounds alike? How were they different?

6. Do you feel called by God to "do life" together? Why?

7. How are you alike in your financial styles? How are you different?

8. Have a financial heart to heart with your beloved. What did you learn?

9. If you are living together, how will marriage change your finances?

10. Why should you tithe? Prepare a financial budget that includes tithing.

11. How has being with your beloved changed you?

Leaving and Cleaving

12. Which statement in this section was the most helpful to you? Why?

13. Which of the scripture verses quoted in this section is your favorite? Why?

14. What challenge are you most likely to face with your parents?

15. What challenge are you most likely to face with your in-laws?

The Marriage Bed

16. Which statement in this section was the most helpful to you? Why?

17. Which of the scripture verses quoted in this section is your favorite? Why?

18. What romantic thing(s) has your beloved done for you?

19. What do you find sexy about your beloved?

Lesson #6: Handling Anger & Conflict

(Love) is not *easily* angered. 1 Corinthians 13:5 (NIV)

Notice that Paul does *not* say that love never gets angry. He says that love doesn't get angry easily. There is a world of difference in those two statements. Most of you probably think that anytime you get angry, you have failed to love. But that's not what the Bible says.

You see, anger and love are not necessarily incompatible. In fact, the Bible tells us that even Jesus got angry in certain circumstances. Once, the disciples tried to prevent little children from getting through to see Jesus, thinking they were unimportant to his work.

> When Jesus saw this, he became *angry* and said, "Let the children come to me! Don't try to *stop* them. People who are like these little children *belong* to the kingdom of God. Mark 10:14 (CEV)

Another time, some religious leaders objected to Jesus' healing on the Sabbath, preferring to hold onto their arcane rules about work on the Sabbath—while violating the spirit and meaning of God's Sabbath commandment.

> He looked around at them in *anger* and, deeply distressed at their *stubborn hearts*, said to the man, "Stretch out your hand." He stretched it out, and his hand was completely *restored*. Mark 3:5 (NIV)

You see, in certain circumstances anger is an entirely normal and healthy emotion for you to feel. God uses anger to alert you to the fact that something is wrong in your relational world, much like he uses pain to alert you that something is wrong in your physical body. At the core of your anger is the belief that you or someone you care about has been wronged.

Contrary to popular belief, it's not your anger that gets you into trouble with others. It's how you express your anger that alienates others, and that undermines your love for them. You see, you can choose to express your anger in an undisciplined, self-centered, and destructive manner. Or you can choose to express your anger in a loving, constructive way. It's entirely your choice.

> When you are *angry*, do not *sin*. Psalm 4:4 (NCV)

Instead of trying not to be angry, you should put your energy into learning how to make your anger a constructive force for good.

The Constructive Use of Anger

➤ Learn to recognize your anger

> Better a patient man than a warrior, a man who *controls* his *temper* than one who takes a city. Proverbs 16:32 (NIV)

Most people don't become aware that they are angry until it is too late for them to control themselves. Once your anger has reached the boiling point, once you have reached your limit, once you have exploded in anger and frustration, or once you have withdrawn in icy silence, there is little you can do to control your anger or to channel it in constructive ways.

If you want to be successful in controlling your anger, you need to learn to recognize your anger early on, when it first begins to tug at your heart. The earlier you recognize that you are angry about something, the better you can control your response to the thing that angers you. Moreover, your response will be more constructive because you will be less emotional and more objective in your judgment, better able to consider various points of view and alternative solutions, more gracious in your attitude, and more tactful in what you say.

Those of you who have been taught that anger is "bad" have a particularly difficult time recognizing when you are angry. You are conditioned to ignore angry feelings because you don't want to be a bad person. Rather than deal with your anger while it is still manageable, you allow your anger to simmer and grow, unacknowledged and unchecked, until it pours out of you. Even then, some of you will deny that you are angry.

Don't *sin* by letting anger gain *control* over you. Psalm 4:4 (NLT)

Unrecognized anger typically begins with a sense of generalized agitation. In other words, you may be upset (Mes), stirred up (NIV), or in turmoil (GN) about all sorts of little things because you are afraid to acknowledge that you are angry about something. You try to ignore your angry feelings—to stuff them—but the anger seeps out of you as generalized irritability, agitation, unsettledness, and turmoil.

Mockers can get a whole town *agitated*, but those who are wise will *calm* anger. Proverbs 29:8 (NLT)

Compounding your difficulty in recognizing your anger is the fact people express their anger in different, but equally destructive, ways.

Loud anger is what we typically think of as anger. It yells, it rants and raves, it explodes, and it spews its venom all over anyone unfortunate enough to get in its way. Only about 23% of you openly express your anger in a loud way, according to a survey by Bernice Kanner.[1] Your loud, destructive way of expressing your anger gets you into a lot of arguments, causes you to say and do things you ought not to, and damages your relationships with others.

A person with a *quick* temper stirs up *arguments* and commits a lot of sins. Proverbs 29:22 (CEV)

But not everyone vents when they are angry. Most of you (approximately 39% in the survey) try to contain your anger. You try to hide it. You bottle it up. And because you are quiet on the outside, you think you're handling your anger. You think you're not angry. But "stuffing it" on the outside doesn't do anything about the anger inside of you. Your repressed anger doesn't go away; it expresses itself through sarcasm, resentment, disrespect, and aloofness.

So I kept very *quiet*...but I became even more *upset*. I became very angry *inside*, and as I thought about it, my anger burned. Psalm 39:2-3 (NCV)

Some of you simply walk away from angry situations (approximately 23% in the survey). You try to avoid situations in which people express anger. You may think that you are taking the high road. You may commend yourself for refusing to "stoop to their level." In reality, your avoidance of angry situations is probably rooted in your fear of them. Based upon your past experiences, especially in childhood, you have come to believe that only bad things can happen when people get angry. You solution is to run away from angry situations. And yet your avoidance does nothing to resolve the anger. It only allows it to fester.

> My thoughts are *troubled*…because my loud enemies shout and attack. They treat me terribly and hold angry grudges. My heart is *racing fast*…I am trembling with *fear*, completely terrified. Psalm 55:2-5 (CEV)

➤ Don't allow yourself to vent

When you are angry, it is important not to lose sight of your purpose. As we have seen, anger is an indicator that something is wrong in your relational world. When you are confronted with evil or injustice or brokenness in your world, whether it be in the public arena or in your private life, your anger motivates you to right the wrong.

> The *anger* of the Lord will not turn back until he fully accomplishes the *purposes* of his heart. Jeremiah 23:20 (NIV)

In this instance, God was angry with his chosen people, the nation of Israel, because they had forsaken him for other gods. But God did allow himself to "vent." If God had let his anger burn unchecked, he would have wiped Israel off the face of the earth. He would have been justified in doing so, but he would have totally defeated the purpose of his anger, which was turning Israel away from idol worship.

Anger must always be controlled in order to accomplish its purpose. When anger is uncontrolled, it ends up destroying the very thing it seeks. In this example, God controlled his anger by handing over Israel into captivity in Babylon instead of annihilating them. And the Babylonian captivity permanently seared the conscience of Israel so that they never again worshipped idols.

Either you control your anger or your anger controls you. It's your choice. But if you want your anger to end constructively, if you want to right the wrong that makes you angry, and if you hope to fix the underlying problem, you must choose to control your anger.

> A *fool* gives full *vent* to his anger, but a wise man keeps himself under *control*. Proverbs 29:11 (NIV)

If you allow yourself to focus on how angry you are, and if you aren't careful about the words you say, you will end up saying all sorts of things you had resolved never to say. You will say anything you need to say (no matter how destructive) in order to win the argument. You will make the problem worse. In fact, your angry words and your angry behavior may create a whole new set of problems.

> The *more* talk, the less truth; the wise *measure* their words. Proverbs 10:19 (Mes)

There are many things that can happen when you lose your temper, but none of them are good. If you allow yourself to vent, you shouldn't expect a good outcome. In fact, losing your temper is one of the most stupid and counterproductive things you can do.

> It's smart to be patient, but it's *stupid* to lose your *temper*. Proverbs 14:29 (CEV)

Giving full vent to your anger only produces more anger.[2] When you rant and rave, your body churns up more anger, and you begin to think of additional reasons to be angry. The wrong grows bigger and bigger in your eyes. You see, "pouring out" your anger doesn't help you get rid of your anger; it just makes you more angry.

> Just as *stirring* milk makes butter…so stirring up *anger* causes *trouble*. Proverbs 30:33 (NCV)

When you are angry, you need to choose your advisors very carefully. Don't seek out an angry person, someone you know will agree with you and help pump up your anger into righteous indignation.

> *Keep away* from angry, short-tempered people, or you will learn to be *like* them and endanger your *soul*. Proverbs 22:24-25 (NLT)

Instead, seek out someone you know will calm you down, someone who will encourage you to keep your anger under control. Seek out the person who can help you identify the root cause or purpose of your anger, who can help put the offense into perspective, and who can suggest constructive ways to resolve the problem.

A hot-tempered man stirs up strife, but the *slow* to anger *calms* a dispute. Proverbs 15:18 (NAS)

➤ Double-check your facts

Your anger is always based on the belief that something is wrong in your relational world, that you or someone you care about has been wronged. Therefore, it is very important to make sure that you've got your facts straight, that your perception is accurate, and that the wrong you seek to right actually exists.

> Be *careful* what you think, because your *thoughts* run your life. Proverbs 4:23 (NCV)

Whenever you are first presented with a situation that seems unfair, you probably don't have all the facts. In fact, it can take quite a while for all the relevant information to come to light. This is why you should be slow to become angry and why you must not jump to conclusions.

> Everyone should be *quick* to listen, slow to speak, and *slow* to become angry. James 1:19 (NIV)

Things are not always as they seem. In the parable of the Prodigal Son, the older brother got angry because he thought his father was being unfair. He assumed that because his father celebrated the younger brother's return, he would ignore the consequences of his son's misbehavior. In comparison, he felt that his father slighted his own years of service.

> The older brother was *angry*…"All these years I've worked hard for you and never once refused to do a single thing you told me to. And in all that time you never gave *me* even one young goat for a feast with my friends. Yet when this son of yours comes back after *squandering* your money on prostitutes, you *celebrate* by killing the finest calf we have." Luke 15:28-30 (NLT)

The older brother got angry because he underestimated his father. His father's joy at the younger brother's repentance and return did not mean that he would rescue him from the consequences of his behavior. The older brother's faithfulness would be rewarded, because everything remaining in the father's estate would go to him.

His father said, "Son, you don't *understand*. You're with me all the time, and *everything* that is mine is *yours*—but this is a wonderful time, and we had to celebrate. This brother of yours…was lost, and he's found!" Luke 15:31-32 (Mes)

If you want to use your anger constructively, you need to make sure you clearly understand the situation before you respond to it. When something seems unfair to you, you will almost always need to gather more information and to ask questions about the intent of the person you are angry with.

However, when you are angry, asking questions can be tricky. Unless you are very careful, you will end up making accusations instead of asking honest questions. You see, you must not accuse the person you are angry with of having evil or malicious motives. You must be willing to give the person the benefit of the doubt. You must entertain the possibility that you misunderstood something or that they made an honest mistake.

➢ Check your worldview if you are chronically angry

Anger is an emotion you should experience only occasionally, like pain. Chronic anger, like chronic pain, indicates that something is seriously out of kilter. God never made you to live with extended patterns of anger. Chronic anger is destructive to your physical body,[3] and it is extremely destructive to your relationships.[4]

In the same way that anger indicates that something is wrong in your relational world, chronic anger indicates that something is wrong with your basic assumptions about the way things are. When anger becomes your primary emotional response to the things that happen in your world, your worldview is faulty. Your general perception of life, the meaning you assign to events, and the motives you attribute to others, are all seriously distorted.

The emotional lens through which you view your world should be trust and hope. However, if you are chronically angry, you may unconsciously believe that life is stacked against you, that everyone is out to get you, that you can never get ahead, and that life is always and ultimately unfair. Your emotional lens will be distorted because, as the scripture says, you have exchanged the truth of God for a lie.

They exchanged the *truth* of God for a *lie*. Romans 1:25 (NIV)

The source of these lies and deceptions is none other than that ancient enemy, Satan. Satan wants to destroy you and to take you down with himself. He wants to separate you from God. He has no conscience, and he has no scruples.

> The *thief* comes only in order to *steal, kill,* and *destroy.* I have come in order that you might have life—life in all its fullness. John 10:10 (GN)

Whenever you show any weakness, Satan bombards you with thoughts filled with half-truths and outright lies. He will twist God's words in order to make God seem uncaring or unfair. He will accuse you unjustly in order to discourage and defeat you. He feels no shame in exploiting your greatest vulnerabilities.

> That ancient *serpent,* named the Devil, or Satan, that *deceived* the whole world...the one who stood before our God and *accused* believers day and night. Revelation 12:9-10 (GN)

In the Garden, God told Adam that he could eat fruit from all the trees except one particular tree whose fruit would cause him to die. Later, Satan came to Eve and misquoted God's instructions, twisting God's words to make him seem unfair.

> Did God tell you *not* to eat fruit from *any* tree in the garden? Genesis 3:1 (CEV)

Then Satan lied to her, denying that eating the fruit would cause her to die.

> That's *not* true; you will not *die.* Genesis 3:4 (GN)

Finally, Satan told Eve a half-truth. After she ate the fruit, her eyes *were* opened to good and evil, but instead of being like God, she got spiritual death and physical death.

> God knows that your eyes will be *opened* when you eat it. You will become *just like God,* knowing everything, both good and evil. Genesis 3:5 (NLT)

Now, some of you had parents who failed or abandoned you. Some of your lives have had more than their fair share of hard knocks or injustice. When this is the case, Satan has plenty of bad stuff from your past to throw at you. Moreover, his lies and half-truths can be particularly difficult for you to recognize and reject because they seem to reflect the reality of your personal experience.

That is why it is so important to know God and to let him work in your life. As you grow in your knowledge of God, both from the scriptures and experientially as you follow him, you will grow in your confidence of God's love for you.

You will be better able to recognize Satan's lies and half-truths. You see, no matter what happened in your past, the world is not stacked against you.

> I can do *all things* through Christ, because he *gives* me strength. Philippians 4:13 (NCV)

No matter how critical or abusive or manipulative the adults in your life have been, God does not accuse you. He is rooting for you to succeed!

> If God is *for* us, who can be *against* us?...*Who* is he that condemns? Romans 8:31-34 (NIV)

➢ Release your worries to God

Feelings of anxiety and worry often spill out in angry words.

> Don't give in to *worry* or *anger*; it only leads to trouble. Psalms 37:8 (GN)

You see, when you are anxious about something that is going on in your world, or when you are worried about making things work out, or when you are insecure in a certain relationship, your emotional tank may be running on empty. Stress does that to you. Worry and anxiety deplete you emotionally.

Self-control requires adequate emotional resources. When your emotional tank runs out of gas, it is almost impossible to be patient, to be concerned about the needs of others, and to be hopeful about the future. Anger inevitably spills out because you don't have the emotional resources to hold yourself together any longer.

Your anger may seem to come out of left field, shocking both yourself and those around you. The tenor of your response may seem completely inappropriate to the matter at hand. In fact, your anger may have nothing to do with the current situation, but everything to do with your anxiety about something else.

In these situations, you need to ask yourself some diagnostic questions. Is there something in your life that you are anxious about that is producing this misplaced anger? Do you feel insecure in your marriage or that you are losing out to a career, to the kids, to a hobby? Are you worried about something at work? Are you worried about money? Are you worried about someone's health? Remember, God never intended you to live with worry.

Do not *worry* about your *life*, what you will eat or drink; or about your body, what you will wear. Matthew 6:25 (NIV)

God wants to care for you like a father cares for his children. He wants to provide everything you need. He wants to help you carry your burdens. However, he cannot do so unless you commit your needs to his care and release your worries to him.

Sometimes that outburst of anger is an indicator that you need to stop stewing about something, and you need to stop nursing your anxieties. You need to pray about it instead. You need to commit the thing that is worrying you to God's care.

Don't *worry* about anything; instead, *pray* about everything. Tell God what you need, and *thank* him for all he has done. Philippians 4:6 (NLT)

By thanking God for what he has done for you and others in the past, you build your faith. You put your problems into perspective. You fill up your emotional tank with the confidence that God loves you and that he is more than able to take care of you. Then God's supernatural peace will settle on you, displacing all your anger.

God will bless you with *peace* that no one can completely *understand*. And this peace will *control* the way you think and feel. Philippians 4:7 (CEV)

➤ Be flexible in your expectations

In any situation, you have expectations about what you think will happen. In fact, your response to what actually happens is largely determined by the expectations you had. If the situation turns out better than you had expected, you will be pleasantly surprised or perhaps even overjoyed.

They went *beyond* our highest *hopes*, for their first action was to dedicate themselves to the Lord and to us for *whatever* directions God might give them. 2 Corinthians 8:5 (NLT)

But if the reality of the situation fails to meet your expectations, you will be disappointed.

A man had a *fig* tree planted in his vineyard. He came *looking* for some fruit on the tree, but he found *none*. Luke 13:6 (NCV)

Sometimes there is nothing wrong with your expectations. After all, if you plant a fig tree, you do so in order to harvest figs. But life is full of surprises. You may be disappointed even when your expectations are reasonable.

Disappointment frequently spills out as anger, particularly when you feel wronged or betrayed by what happened. And the greater your disappointment—the greater the distance between the reality of the situation and your expectation of it—the greater you anger will be.

> They *expected* to receive *more*. But each one of them also received a denarius. When they received it, they began to *grumble* against the landowner. Matthew 20:10-11 (NIV)

How do you respond when you are disappointed? Do you grumble because your expectations were not met? Do you get angry? Do you explode? Do you bottle up your anger?

How should you respond to disappointment? First, remember that disappointments are part of life. Nothing is going to be perfect. Second, understand that God's underlying purpose for you is to make you more like himself. God is much more interested in shaping your character than in meeting your expectations. He can use any situation, no matter how good or how bad, how thrilling or how disappointing, to make good things happen inside of you.

> We also have *joy* with our *troubles*, because we know that these troubles produce patience. And patience produces *character*, and character produces hope. Romans 5:3-4 (NCV)

You can have hope in a disappointing situation if you are willing to replace your point of view with God's point of view. Ask God to give you new expectations for the situation, expectations that match up with his purposes. When your expectations come from God, you will not be disappointed. You will feel loved.

> And this *expectation* will not *disappoint* us. For we know how dearly God *loves* us, because he has given us the Holy Spirit to fill our hearts with his love. Romans 5:5 (NLT)

Another way you can meet your disappointment head on is to focus on the good in the situation. It may take you a while to adjust your point of view, but no situation is without its blessings. Find the good things that are present and dwell on those things.

> Whatever is *true*, whatever is noble, whatever is right, whatever is pure, whatever is lovely, whatever is admirable—if anything is *excellent* or praiseworthy—*think* about such things. Philippians 4:8 (NIV)

Every rose bush has thorns. You can either put your emotional energy into being angry at the thorns, or you can put your emotional energy into enjoying the roses. You can't do both.

➢ Actively seek resolution

You are not helpless in the face of anger. You have a choice about how you will respond to circumstances and events that make you angry. You can choose to express your anger in constructive words and actions in an attempt to fix what is wrong. Or, you can choose to express your anger destructively in hurtful words (or to withdraw in resentful silence).

Take responsibility for yourself. Don't blame other people for your angry outbursts. Don't blame circumstances, either. You are the one who chooses how you will respond, so don't play the blame game. Search your own heart when you are tempted to vent your anger.

> In your *anger* do not sin; when you are on your beds, *search* your hearts and be silent. Psalm 4:4 (NIV)

Learn to control what you say. And learn to think before you speak. An undisciplined tongue can get you into all sorts of trouble.

> If anyone considers himself religious and yet does not keep a *tight rein* on his tongue, he *deceives* himself and his religion is *worthless*. James 1:26 (NIV)

As we have seen, your words have power. Angry words simply churn out more anger. Unchecked, your angry words can take over your life, propelling you in directions you never intended.

> The *tongue* is a flame of fire. It is full of *wickedness* that can ruin your whole life. It can *turn* the entire course of your life into a blazing flame of destruction. James 3:6 (NLT)

Some people get very angry over little things—over things of no real consequence. They are quick to take offense where none was intended. These are the people that others "walk on eggshells" around, because it doesn't take much to set them off.

In contrast, you can choose to be slow to take offense. You can choose to give people the benefit of the doubt in awkward situations. You can treat them as people of good will, whose intentions were good even when the outcome is unfortunate. You can even choose to ignore provocations and insults, keeping your focus on the substantive issues between you.

> A *fool* shows his *annoyance* at once, but a prudent man *overlooks* an insult. Proverbs 12:16 (NIV)

Take the initiative to resolve your anger. Reach out to the person you are angry with. When others are angry with you, reach out to them. Try to resolve the problem between you and to restore your relationship. Whenever it is possible, resolve the problem on the very same day it crops up.

> Do not let the *sun go down* on your anger. Ephesians 4:26 (NAS)

If you refuse to reach out to others when you are angry, you risk getting stuck in bitterness. Bitterness is frozen rage; it is anger that retreats into an icy silence. You refuse to talk about the problem because you'd rather nurse your feelings of outrage than try to restore your relationship. Ironically, bitter people think of themselves as helpless victims. They hold onto their anger in an attempt to punish those who have "wronged" them. But they end up destroying themselves instead.

> Get rid of all *bitterness, rage* and *anger*. Ephesians 4:31 (NIV)

The Constructive Use of Conflict

> It is better to live in a *corner* of a roof than in a house shared with a *contentious* woman. Proverbs 21:9 (NAS)

Not a pretty picture, is it? Some of you are very uncomfortable with the idea of conflict in your marriage. When you picture yourself being happily married, you picture a marriage without conflict. In fact, your concept of becoming one with your spouse in marriage is that you two will see eye to eye on every subject, you will never have a disagreement, you will always mystically want the very same things, and you will be blissfully happy.

Get real! That's not how life works. Conflict is inevitable in life. Because God has made you individuals, it is inevitable that you will have different points of view.

These differences are part of the strength of marriage. The reason that "two heads are better than one" is because there are two different points of view that can balance one another. This is part of God's design. Remember that he created male and female brains to be innately drawn to different aspects of the world around them. You can expect that you will routinely have different priorities than your spouse, simply because God made you aware of different things in your world.

The frequency of conflict between spouses has no bearing on their happiness in marriage. Their happiness depends instead upon how successfully they are able to resolve their conflicts. In fact, successful couples are able to resolve their differences in ways that actually strengthen their relationships and improve their intimacy.

In contrast, the avoidance of conflict is the number one predictor of divorce.[5] Couples who are determined to avoid conflict and who habitually avoid discussing their disagreements with one another end up with "irreconcilable differences" because they never make any attempt to resolve them.

➤ Try to see the opportunity for good

Conflict does not have to be negative. Every conflict has the potential to be a learning experience, a turning point, and an opportunity for good. It is how you handle the conflict that determines whether your disagreement will have a positive or negative outcome.

Example #1: During the Lord's Supper, the disciples began to argue with one another about which one of them was the most important disciple. Unfortunately, it was an argument they had had before.

> An *argument* broke out among the *disciples* as to which one of them should be thought of as the *greatest*. Luke 22:24 (GN)

Jesus took their argument as an opportunity to teach them about the responsibilities of leadership. He wanted them to understand that he had chosen them not to lord it over others, but to serve them.

But among you, those who are the *greatest* should take the lowest rank, and the *leader* should be like a *servant*. Luke 22:26 (NLT)

Example #2: Jesus and the disciples were Jewish and followed Jewish laws of religious observance. Early church leaders disagreed with each other about whether Gentile believers should be required to follow Jewish law as well.

Some men came from Judea to Antioch and started *teaching* the believers, "You cannot be saved unless you are *circumcised* as the Law of Moses requires." Paul and Barnabas got into a fierce *argument* with them about this. Acts 15:1-2 (GN)

God used their disagreement as an opportunity to clarify and build consensus concerning fundamental church doctrine. The church council at Jerusalem determined that salvation for everyone was through faith in Christ Jesus and his sacrifice (and not through external acts or observance of Jewish law) after Peter and Paul recounted God's miraculous work among the Gentile believers and James quoted scripture that foretold God's plan to redeem the Gentiles.

Now then, why do you try to test God by putting on the necks of the disciples a *yoke* that neither we nor our fathers have been able to bear? No! We believe it is through the *grace* of our Lord Jesus that we are *saved*, just as they are. Acts 15:10-11 (NIV)

Example #3: Paul and Barnabas argued about whether they should take John Mark along on their next missionary journey.

Barnabas wanted to *take* John, also called Mark, with them, but Paul *did not* think it wise to take him, because he had *deserted* them in Pamphylia. Acts 15:37-38 (NIV)

When Paul was a new convert, Barnabus took him under his wing. For several years, they served together as an effective missionary team. But God used their disagreement over John Mark as a turning point to launch Paul out into ministry on his own. As a result, two missionary teams were sent forth instead of just one.

They had such a sharp *disagreement* that they *parted* company. Barnabas took Mark and sailed for Cyprus, but Paul chose Silas and left. Acts 15:39-40 (NIV)

➢ **Work together for resolution**

Not all conflict is created equal. Mark Cummings has identified four types of marital conflict in his work with children.[6]

Destructive conflict occurs when there is verbal and physical aggression between the partners (in essence just the uncontrolled venting of anger) that causes the conflict to remain unresolved.

> A brother who has been insulted is harder to win back than a *walled city*, and *arguments* separate people like the *barred gates* of a palace. Proverbs 18:19 (NCV)

Destructive conflict between parents results in a negative outcome for their children. Children become distressed, sad, angry and fearful, and they are very sensitive to any form of conflict. They show increased aggression, anxiety, emotional insecurity, and depression, and experience greater difficulty in school and in peer relationships.

Nonverbal conflict occurs when the partners withdraw from one another, stonewall, and show disrespect toward each other. Parents tend to think that they are hiding their conflict from their children, but children are very sensitive to the emotional quality of the home. They are just as upset when the unresolved conflict is nonverbal, and they experience the same negative outcomes.

Productive conflict occurs when problems are calmly shared and discussed, but not resolved.

> A *gentle* answer will *calm* a person's anger, but an unkind answer will cause more anger. Proverbs 15:1 (NCV)

Productive conflict between parents results in a neutral outcome for their children. Children are not troubled by the conflict, but neither are they uplifted by it.

Constructive conflict occurs when problems are resolved and everyday family functioning improves as a result of the conflict.

> The *tongue* of the wise makes knowledge *acceptable*. Proverbs 15:2 (NAS)

Constructive conflict between parents results in a positive outcome for their children. Children report feeling uplifted when they observe their parents handling conflict in a constructive manner. They show increased social competency and emotional security. In addition, they are not distressed when conflict occurs.[7]

How frequently parents experience conflict does not seem to matter.[8] How the parents express their disagreements and whether they are able to resolve the conflict between them determines whether the children are affected positively or negatively.

Your attitude toward conflict was formed by type of conflict you observed between your parents as a child. If your childhood home was full of destructive conflict, you may fear all types of conflict and view any disagreements between you and your spouse as potential disasters. If you experienced productive conflict as a child, you will not fear conflict. But if you grew up in a home with constructive conflict, you will view it as an opportunity for improving your marriage and deepening your relationship with your spouse.

You did not get to choose the type of home you grew up in, but you do get to choose the type of marriage you will have. Resolve together that you will handle your conflicts constructively. Simply avoiding the conflict between you will cause your relationship to be more fragile and more superficial.

➢ Choose a productive time

If either of you is struggling to control your anger, you would do well to give yourselves a time-out to calm down and gain some perspective. Unless you do so, you are not likely to be able to discuss the issue constructively.

> *Losing* your temper causes a lot of trouble, but staying calm *settles* arguments.
> Proverbs 15:18 (CEV)

You can say something like, "I want to resolve this issue, but right now I'm struggling to control my emotions and I need some time to get my thoughts together." Then go do something that helps you relax and gives you time to think. You need to begin praying, asking God to help you clear your thoughts, sort out your emotions, and see things from his perspective. You will know when you have gained God's perspective because you will be filled with peace and hope. Then you can go back to your spouse and discuss your conflict constructively.

> Good people *think before* they answer, but the wicked simply *pour* out evil.
> Proverbs 15:28 (NCV)

If either of you is physically tired, you would do well to postpone your discussion until you have had a chance to get some rest. Problems always seem bigger and conflict always seems worse when you are tired. This is a real problem in our culture because most of us live in a chronic state of exhaustion.

When you are physically tired, you are emotionally depleted as well. You won't have the emotional resiliency to face new problems or to give the other person the benefit of the doubt. If you try to discuss a disagreement, you will be only one mis-statement away from the proverbial straw that breaks the camel's back. You see, when you are exhausted, you are never far from an emotional melt-down.

Elijah was a mighty prophet of God. After he successfully confronted and destroyed the prophets of Baal, his life was threatened by Queen Jezebel. Elijah fled into the desert. But after walking all day, he was physically exhausted and emotionally spent.

> Elijah was *afraid* and ran for his life…He came to a broom tree, sat down under it and prayed that he might *die*. 1 Kings 19:3-4 (NIV)

In order to avoid such a melt-down, you should say something like, "I want to discuss this, but right now I'm too tired to talk. Let's wait until (*time*) when I can think more clearly and less emotionally." Make sure you take a nap or get a good night's sleep to replenish your energy levels. Then you can discuss the conflict constructively.

Time of day can play a significant role in conflict, too. If you are not a morning person, don't try to resolve a conflict first thing in the morning. Similarly, if your spouse isn't a morning person, don't bring up something that bothers you over breakfast. In addition, if the energy levels of either you or your spouse drop precipitously in the late afternoon, you should avoid serious discussions until after dinner. Or if you turn into a pumpkin at night, don't try to discuss anything important just before bed.

Finally, if your spouse is busy or preoccupied, don't choose that time to bring up bad news or potential conflicts. Wait until your spouse is relaxed and can give you his/her full attention. No one likes to be ambushed. Your discussion can wait for a more opportune time. Be smart; give yourself a chance for constructive dialog.

➢ Develop empathy for your spouse

If you wish to resolve your conflict successfully, you must come to understand that your spouse is not your enemy. You two are on the same team. Your enemy is the problem between you that seeks to tear you apart. If you are in an argumen-tative mood, you need to shift gears and adopt a problem-solving mind-set.

> Some people make *cutting* remarks, but the words of the wise bring *healing*.
> Proverbs 12:18 (NIV)

You must be able to treat your spouse with respect. Put aside your anger and your desire to lash out at your spouse, to belittle him/her, or to demonstrate your spouse's "stupidity." Your attitude is key in showing respect, because you can be harsh or sarcastic without ever raising your voice. Instead, be gentle with your spouse.

> A *gentle* response diffuses anger, but a *sharp tongue* kindles a temper-fire. Proverbs 15:1 (Mes)

Whenever you are discussing the conflict, choose your words very carefully. Don't make inflammatory statements. Avoid words that imply negative behavior or motives on your spouse's part. Just because your spouse has a different point of view does not mean that he/she is being unreasonable.

> The heart of the righteous *ponders* how to *answer*, but the mouth of the wicked pours out evil things. Proverbs 15:28 (NAS)

Your first goal in discussing the conflict is to develop a sympathetic understanding of your spouse's point of view. Forget trying to fix blame for the problem or trying to justify yourself. Neither will move you toward the resolution of the conflict, but understanding your spouse's point of view will.

> Fools have no interest in *understanding*; they only want to *air* their own *opinions*. Proverbs 18:2 (NLT)

Try to understand the conflict as your spouse sees it. What is your spouse's analysis of the problem? How are the issues framed in his/her mind? What aspect is most troubling to your spouse about the problem? What are his/her criteria for a satisfactory solution, and how does your spouse suggest that the problem be solved? Imagine how you would think and feel if you were in your spouse's place. Consider how the solution you are proposing will affect your spouse, what the consequences are for him/her. This is the **cognitive component** of empathy.

> Be of one mind, full of *sympathy* toward each other, loving one another with *tender* hearts and *humble* minds. 1 Peter 3:8 (NLT)

In addition, do not diminish your spouse's feelings of distress; take them seriously. It is not enough to understand *why* your spouse feels the way he/she does; you need to imagine how your spouse feels and to feel something of the emotions he/she feels. In other words, your heart should go out to your spouse in his/her distress. This is the **emotional component** of empathy.

> So, as those who have been chosen of God, holy and beloved, put on a *heart* of *compassio*n. Colossians 3:12 (NAS)

As you seek to develop empathy for your spouse, you need to give him/her your full attention. Maintain eye contact and listen carefully to his/her words. Watch for nonverbal cues that might indicate that your spouse's words don't reflect his/her true feelings. You see, until your spouse feels "understood" by you, you won't be able to resolve the problem between you.

Your greatest difficulty in resolving a conflict is getting to the point that each of you is emotionally *willing* to resolve the conflict. The spiritual battle you must fight involves getting yourselves past the blame game, your old fears, the need to defend yourself, and mistrust of each other's motives. Empathy can help you get there.

➢ Seek an unexpected solution

Once you are able to join hands as allies against your common problem, the resolution of conflict can begin. You will not be negotiating with each other in the traditional sense. You are not trying to determine which one of you will win the argument, which one of you will prevail in your opinion, or which one of you was right. Remember, you aren't competitors; you are allies.

Nor will you be seeking compromise as that term is traditionally understood. You will not be trading concessions and trying to merge conflicting points of view. The problem with compromise is that you end up with a solution that nei-ther of you likes very much. Think of the old joke about a giraffe being an animal put together by committee. Each person got something he wanted, but the whole doesn't work together very well. Worse still, your compromise may fail to address the underlying problem behind your conflict.

What you are after is **synthesis**.[9] That is, you will take the presence of conflict between you as evidence that there is a problem to be solved. Then you will take your respective points of view as the starting point in your search for a solution.

In essence, you are brainstorming for a solution that is better than the solution that occurred to either of you initially. By exploring the implications of your respective view points, you will develop a more complete understanding of the problem that is causing the conflict. A better understanding of the problem will lead you to a better and more satisfying solution.

O Lord, *listen* to my cry; give me the *discerning* mind you promised. Psalm 119:169 (NLT)

Ask God for insight. Say, "God, please help us to understand what is really going on here." God will help you identify the root problem which underlies your conflict. You see, sometimes the problem you are arguing about is merely the symptom of a deeper problem. God's enduring purpose is to free you from your sinful nature, and he will use conflict as an opportunity to reveal something in your heart or in your character that needs to be changed.

He will bring to light what is *hidden* in darkness and will *expose* the *motives* of men's hearts. 1 Corinthians 4:5 (NIV)

Then ask God for a solution to the problem. Say, "God, what should we do? What is your provision for this problem?" It is amazing how frequently the germ of a solution will come to mind even before you finish praying. At the very least, praying about a problem together puts it in a different context and helps you to consider options you wouldn't have considered before. Our God is faithful.

God, who has *called* you into fellowship with his Son Jesus Christ our Lord, *is faithful.* 1 Corinthians 1:9 (NIV)

Homework
Lesson #6: Handling Anger & Conflict

The Constructive Use of Anger

1. Which statement in this section was the most helpful to you? Why?

2. Which of the scripture verses quoted in this section is your favorite? Why?

3. Were you taught that anger is bad? Please explain.

4. When angry: Do you vent? Do you get real quiet? Do you try to flee?

5. Have you jumped to a false conclusion when you were angry? Please explain.

6. Ask your beloved. Do your questions turn into accusations when you are angry?

7. Do you unconsciously believe that life is stacked against you? Please explain.

8. Have you released a worry to God? What happened?

9. Are you quick to take offense? To give others the benefit of the doubt?

The Constructive Use of Conflict

10. Which statement in this section was the most helpful to you? Why?

11. Which of the scripture verses quoted in this section is your favorite? Why?

12. Do disagreements make you uncomfortable? Why?

13. Why is productive conflict not enough?

14. What are the best times of the day for your beloved? What are the worst?

15. Have you ever stopped and prayed during an argument? What happened?

16. What happens when you try to justify yourself in an argument?

17. Why is compromise not enough?

18. Give an example of an argument that didn't address the root problem.

Lesson #7: Healing Hurts through Forgiveness

One of the greatest tests of a relationship is how you respond when someone hurts you. Interestingly, it is not the hurt itself that destroys the relationship. Every enduring marriage has weathered its fair share of hurts and miscues.

No marriage is exempt from hurts, and no other relationship is either. Relational hurts occur between parents and children, between siblings, with extended family members, with past romantic liaisons, with authority figures or bosses, with coworkers and friends—in fact, in any human relationship. It is inevitable that hurts come into all relationships, because none of us is perfect. We all make mistakes. Some of our mistakes are intentional, and others are completely unintentional.

If it's not the hurt itself that destroys relationships, what is it that destroys them? It's your response to the hurt. Ask yourself: How do you respond to others when they have hurt you? How do you respond when you think you have been wronged?

Are you **loud**? Do you explode in anger and yell a lot?

Are you **quiet**? Do you become resentful and bitter at the injustice done to you? Do you nurture grudges?

Do you **keep score**? Do you review every hurt that has ever happened in the relationship? Do you store up hurts for future ammunition?

All three of these responses spell disaster, both for you personally and for your relationship. While they may make you feel good about yourself in the short-term (and superior to the offender), they are powerless to heal your hurt. This is the reason the Bible says,

> (Love) doesn't keep a *record* of *wrongs* that others do. 1 Corinthians 13:5 (CEV)

The Bible is very clear; the only way to heal your hurt is to forgive the offender.

> Be kind and compassionate to one another, *forgiving* each other, just as in Christ God *forgave* you. Ephesians 4:32 (NIV)

How do you know that you need to forgive someone? Ask yourself, can you remember the hurt without getting angry or resentful? You see, if you get agitated or are overwhelmed with pain at the memory, then the hurt still controls you. Paradoxically, the way to heal your hurts and move on with your life is not to get even with the offender, but to forgive.

Forgiveness Begins With God

The heart of forgiveness begins in your experience of being forgiven by God. Until you experience being forgiven, you can never forgive others.

➢ Each of us has wronged God

> If we claim to be *without* sin, we *deceive* ourselves. 1 John 1:8 (NIV)

None of us is perfect. We all mess up, in spite of our best intentions. The experience of shame is universal to us. It is God's witness in our hearts of our sin. You see, we can't even measure up to our own standards, much less God's!

> I have the *desire* to do what is good, but I *cannot* carry it out. Romans 7:18 (NIV)

Moreover, there is an emptiness inside of us that persists even when we get what we want, when we achieve our goals, and when we get the things we thought would make us happy. There is a God-shaped hole in our hearts because we were made for fellowship with God!

But God is perfect in every way, and our sin, our imperfectness, offends him. There is no way we can have a relationship with God as we are. It is like trying to mix oil and water, or light and darkness.

> How can *goodness* be a partner with *wickedness*? How can light live with darkness? 2 Corinthians 6:14 (NLT)

Either you are perfect or you aren't. The slightest imperfection is enough to disqualify you. God doesn't grade on the curve. We don't get a pass from him if we manage to do more good than bad in our lives. The scales won't tip our way.

In fact, there is nothing we can do to make it up to God for our imperfections, for our flops, failures, and fumbles, for all the wrong we have ever done toward others, and for our rebellion against God. Nothing. We have no way to make things right with God.

We have nothing to offer as restitution[1] to God because we cannot change ourselves. No matter how many good deeds we do, no matter how hard we try, and no matter how many promises we make, we cannot change our fundamental nature, which is incompatible with God's holy and perfect nature.

> The Good News shows *how* God makes people *right* with himself—that it begins and ends with *faith*. Romans 1:17 (NCV)

➢ Jesus made restitution for you

Although we are unable to make restitution with God for our flops, failures, and fumbles, there is one who is. God himself made restitution for us! Wow.

> But our High Priest (Jesus) offered *himself* to God as one *sacrifice* for sins, good for all time. Hebrews 10:12 (NLT)

Why in the world would Jesus sacrifice himself for us? It cost him dearly, much more than we can ever comprehend. Why couldn't he just ignore our sin? After all, he was God; couldn't he do anything he wanted?

Sin is much too powerful to be ignored. It controls our lives, our emotions, and our thoughts. Sin's power over us had to be broken before we could enter into a relationship with God.

> Yes, when Christ *died*, he died to *defeat* the *power* of sin. Romans 6:10 (NCV)

The only thing in all creation that can defeat the power of sin is the blood of Jesus. Because Jesus is God, his blood is perfect; it is without sin. Because Jesus is God, his blood is all-powerful; it is totally able to defeat the power of sin in our lives.

> He purchased our *freedom* through the *blood* of his Son, and our sins are forgiven. Ephesians 1:7 (NLT)

The new covenant that Jesus established with his disciples during the Last Supper would be sealed by his blood. Jesus willingly died for us, shedding his blood on the cross so that we could have a relationship with God.

> After the supper he took the *cup* and said, "This cup is God's *new covenant,* sealed with my *blood.* Whenever you drink it, do so in memory of me." 1 Corinthians 11:25 (GN)

The only thing we have to offer Jesus is our faith. We have nothing to offer God in restitution for our sins. We can't earn his forgiveness, and we can't change ourselves. The only way we can make things right with God is to rely on Jesus' sacrifice.

> In...*Jesus* there is forgiveness for your sins. Everyone who *believes* in him is *freed* from all guilt and declared *right* with God. Acts 13:38-39 (NLT)

Now, what does it mean to believe in Jesus? It means making Christianity personal, not just subscribing to a set of religious beliefs. You see, it is not enough to believe that Jesus died for everybody's sins; you must believe that he died for *your* sins. It is not enough to believe that God raised Jesus from the grave; you must believe that the resurrected Jesus lives in *you.*

Believing in Jesus means putting your trust in Jesus instead of in yourself. It means accepting God's forgiveness, not because you've worked for it, not because you deserve it, and not because you've promised to turn your life around, but simply because you need it, and because you believe that Jesus can make a difference in your life.

> If we confess our sins to him, he is *faithful* and just to *forgive* us and to *cleanse* us from every wrong. 1 John 1:9 (NLT)

When you come to Jesus with ruthless honesty about yourself and simple trust in him, you will experience a forgiveness that can turn your life around.

➤ God's forgiveness transforms you

When you truly repent of your sins, God comes into your life. His love, his mercy, and his forgiveness pour into you, and when you can hold no more, they spill out to the people around you.

> Repent, then, and *turn* to God, so that your sins may be wiped out, that *times of refreshing* may come from the Lord. Acts 3:19 (NIV)

The experience of God's love—a love that is truly unconditional, that is more than you deserve, and that is utterly reliable—changes the way you think about other people. Moreover, the experience of God's forgiveness—a forgiveness that is able to break the power of sin in your life, that is freely and joyfully given, and that isn't keeping score or holding it over your head—changes the way you respond to the offenses of others.

> He does not treat us as our sins *deserve* or *repay* us according to our iniquities. For as high as the heavens are above the earth, so great is his *love* for those who fear him; as far as the east is from the west, so far has he *removed* our transgressions from us. Psalm 103:10-12 (NIV)

Experiencing God's forgiveness is truly a transformational experience. It changes our thoughts about ourselves and others. That which we have received from God begins to flow out of us to others. Our awareness that we cannot earn God's love and forgiveness and that we have received more than we deserved from God begins to flow out to the people in our relational world.

> *Freely* you have received, *freely* give. Matthew 10:8 (NIV)

In addition, experiencing God's forgiveness makes us aware of the brokenness that underlies all sin. We begin to see past the offenses of others to the hurt and brokenness in their lives. We see the offenders as hurt people needing God, not to excuse their behavior, but to have compassion for them as God has had compassion on us. Experiencing God's forgiveness causes us to see others as God sees them.

> Shouldn't *you* have had mercy on your fellow servant just as *I had* on you? Matthew 18:33 (NIV)

Forgiveness Is In Your Rational Self-Interest

In the Old Testament, God is the only one who forgives. Forgiveness is a divine attribute, used only to restore the relationship between God and his people. There are many commandments about how to bring the right sacrifice to God in order to be forgiven by him. There are many songs that celebrate being forgiven by God. But there is no command anywhere in the Old Testament that instructs people to forgive each other.

The man must bring a ram to the entrance of the sacred tent and give it to a priest, who will then offer it as a *sacrifice* to me, so the man's sins will be *forgiven*. Leviticus 19:21-22 (CEV)

In contrast, Jesus required his disciples to forgive others. In fact, forgiving others for the wrong they had done you became a requirement for receiving God's forgiveness. No longer just the means for restoring the relationship between God and mankind, forgiveness became the means for restoring relationships between people.

Forgive us for doing wrong, as *we forgive* others. Matthew 6:12 (CEV)

Because Jesus lives in you and you participate in his divine nature, you are able to forgive others. Forgiveness may start as an act of your will, but it becomes a reality only as God's heart, his thoughts, and his mercy flow through you.

His *divine power* has given us everything we need for life and godliness...so that through them you may *participate* in the *divine nature* and escape the corruption in the world caused by evil desires. 2 Peter 1:3-4 (NIV)

Jesus wants you to live in freedom from sin, both your own sin and the sin of others. As we have seen, you can break the power that your own sin has in your life by trusting in Jesus' death and his blood. But the only way to break the power that the sins of others have in your life is to forgive them.

➢ Unforgiveness hurts you, not the offender

Unforgiveness punishes you, not the offender. In your mind you may think that by refusing to forgive the offender, you can make him/her suffer and "pay" for the hurt he/she caused you. But when you hold onto your hurt—thinking and stewing over the wrong done to you, nursing the anger and bitterness you feel toward the offender, listing and reviewing the offenses in your mind—who do you think is suffering? It's you, not the offender. Resentment makes *you* miserable.

A stone is *heavy* and sand is weighty, but the *resentment* caused by a fool is *heavier* than both. Proverbs 27:3 (NLT)

Moreover, the offender may be totally unaware of your suffering. That person may be moving on with his/her life, having a ball, oblivious to you. If the offender is a friend or family member, you will be more successful in making him/her aware of your resentment. But instead of making the offender repent, your resentment will drive him/her away from you. Your unforgiveness will end up increasing your hurt instead of fixing it.

That is why unforgiveness is a really stupid strategy for dealing with the hurts that come into your life. It is totally counterproductive. It only increases and perpetuates your hurt. What happened in the past, happened. Nothing can change the past and the hurts or wrongs that you experienced then. All the resentment and bitterness in the world cannot change the past.

Moreover, if you choose to hold onto your hurt and to nurse your resentment, you will find yourself locked in the past. Your focus will be on the offender and the hurt he/she caused. Intellectually and emotionally you will be unable to make choices that help you move on with your life. You'll be stuck in the past, and life will pass you by.

> Can a man take *fire in his bosom* and his clothes not be *burned?* Proverbs 6:27 (NAS)

Even more troubling, we know that whatever we focus on is what we become. Our thoughts determine our behavior. By holding onto the hurts in your life and focusing so much of your attention on the offender, you unwittingly become like him/her. You will develop the negative character qualities of the person who hurt you, even if you consciously try to be the exact opposite.

> Watch out that no *bitter root* of unbelief rises up among you, for whenever it springs up, many are *corrupted* by its *poison.* Hebrews 12:15 (NLT)

Resentments can also get passed on to others, even to succeeding generations long after the fact. In fact, many of the geo-political conflicts in the world today trace their origin to ancient humiliations. The defeat of Serbian forces in 1389 by the Ottoman Turks[2] gave rise to the ancient resentments that have fueled much of the recent violence in Bosnia and Kosovo. Osama bin Laden declared shortly before September 11th that "the tragedy of Andalusia" would not be repeated in Palestine,[3] referring to the southernmost bit of Spain that had slipped from Muslim control when King Ferdinand reclaimed it in 1492. The slaughter of the Muslim defenders of Jerusalem by the Crusaders in 1096[4] still arouses Arab passions when they discuss the current War on Terrorism.

> The fathers have eaten *sour grapes*, and the *children's* teeth are set on edge. Jeremiah 31:29 (NIV)

➤ Take control of your future

Unforgiveness keeps you in the victim role, focused on the wrong that was done to you. As we have seen, you become a prisoner of your past.

But forgiveness puts you back in control because you are able to choose your attitude toward the things that happened to you. You see, you cannot always choose your circumstances in life, but you can always choose your attitude toward those circumstances, and that can make all the difference. As a result, forgiveness lets you embrace the plan that God has for the rest of your life.

Some people think forgiveness means ignoring your hurts, minimizing the wrongs done to you, or pretending that they never happened. It doesn't. Forgiveness means remembering what happened, but choosing the attitude that lets you heal the hurt, break the power of the offense to cause you any more pain, and move on with your life. It is a step of faith toward God.

> Put up with each other, and *forgive* anyone who does you wrong, just as Christ has *forgiven you*. Colossians 3:13 (CEV)

For this reason, the offender's attitude is irrelevant to your decision to forgive. You don't need to wait for the offender to ask for forgiveness before you forgive him/her. Nor does the offender necessarily need to be told of your decision. You forgive for your own benefit, not the offender's. You choose to forgive whenever you are ready to forgive.

> When they came to a place called the Skull, the soldiers crucified Jesus and the criminals...*Jesus* said, "Father, *forgive* them, because they don't *know* what they are *doing*." Luke 23:33-34 (NCV)

There is a myth that says, "to forgive is to forget." That sounds really nice doesn't it? But it is impossible. Your brain records everything that has ever happened to you. Memories may be repressed if they are traumatic. They can be pushed into the background by the multitude of other details and experiences in your life. But your brain doesn't really forget anything.

> I will *forgive* them for the wicked things they did, and I will not *remember* their sins anymore. Hebrews 8:12 (NCV)

This verse does not mean that God literally forgets your sins, that his memory bank is wiped clean, dramatic sermons to that effect notwithstanding. What it means is that the penalty for the sins has been paid by your faith in Jesus. God is no longer holding those sins against you, and he won't ever bring it up to you again.

However, having your sins forgiven does not mean that the consequences of your sin magically go away. The consequences of your sin remain, and God uses those consequences to help you grow into the person he has planned for you to be. In the same way, when you forgive someone, the offender is still accountable for the consequences of his/her sin.

> No one makes a fool of God. What a person *plants*, he will *harvest*. Galatians 6:7 (Mes)

➤ Forgive so that you may be forgiven

One reason you need to forgive others is because one day you're going to need them to forgive you. It's just human nature for others respond to you in like kind. We tend to be kind to those who are kind to us, rude to those who are rude to us, and so on.

> *Stop* judging others, and *you* will not be judged. Stop criticizing others, or it will all come *back* on you. If you forgive others, you will be forgiven. Luke 6:37 (NLT)

But more than that, there is the spiritual principle that God gives to you according to the standard you show to others. Therefore, the measure of forgiveness you give to others is the measure of forgiveness you receive from God.

> Give to others, and God will give to you. Indeed, you will receive a *full measure*, a generous helping…The measure *you use* for others is the one that *God will use* for you. Luke 6:38 (GN)

Jesus was very explicit about this. Once you have experienced God's forgiveness and entered into a relationship with him, you must forgive others if you want God to continue to forgive you. Wow. Does that seem harsh to you?

> If you forgive those who sin against you, your heavenly Father will forgive you. But if you *refuse to forgive* others, your Father will *not forgive your sins*. Matthew 6:14-15 (NLT)

Jesus knows that an unforgiving heart is an unrepentant heart. Conversely, someone who is meek and willing to accept correction is also forgiving of the flops, failures, and fumbles of other people. Your unwillingness to forgive others for the hurt they have caused you is an indicator that your heart is hard, not only toward them but also toward God. You need a soft heart toward God, a repentant heart, in order to receive God's forgiveness.

> When you are *praying*, if you are *angry* with someone, *forgive* him so that your Father in heaven will also forgive your sins. Mark 11:25 (NCV)

God wants you to have a tender heart.

Working through Forgiveness

➢ Don't cheapen forgiveness

Some people use forgiveness for all kinds of things that they shouldn't be using it for. Life is full of irritations and inconveniences that aren't offenses against you; they're just part of life. And when you encounter them, you need to practice patience, not forgiveness. When others don't measure up to your expectations or they do not behave in the way you think they ought, they have not wronged you. You do not need to forgive them; you need to cut them some slack. You need to be patient with them. You see, each irritation or unexpected delay is an opportunity for God to work his character into you.

> Lead a life worthy of your *calling*, for you have been called by God. Be humble and gentle. Be *patient* with each other, making *allowance* for each other's faults because of your love. Ephesians 4:1-2 (NLT)

Remember that just because you experience pain does not mean that someone has wronged you. If you have financial problems, you may feel pain when a coworker gets a big promotion, but that coworker has not wronged you. If you have suffered pregnancy loss, you may feel pain when someone invites you to a baby shower, but that person has not wronged you. It is entirely unreasonable and self-centered to expect others to filter their good news because of the pain in your life. In fact, you need to stir your faith, and allow God to deal with your envy.

Save forgiveness for the big stuff. Learn to accept the routine annoyances and disappointments of life with patience and grace.

A second thing: forgiveness is only appropriate when you are the victim of the offense. You can't forgive an offender for other people's hurts. You can pray for the situation (for both the victim and the offender) but forgiveness isn't yours to give.

In America today, a lot of people like to offer blanket forgiveness for everyone, everywhere. Whenever some tragedy strikes, like when a murderer goes on a rampage, some well-meaning Christians show up with signs that proclaim, "We forgive you." There is only one problem: these sign-bearers don't have the right to forgive because they aren't the victims. In their desire to give a Christian witness, they cheapen forgiveness.

You see, there is no power in forgiving someone who hasn't wronged you. It doesn't cost you a thing. The power of forgiveness comes only after the victims have wrestled with their hurt; and, out of the crucible of their pain, they freely choose to forgive the offender because of the forgiveness they have experienced from God.

➢ Allow yourself time to grieve

Forgiveness does not minimize the hurt. Forgiveness doesn't mutter, "It was no big deal. Don't worry about it. No problem." Instead, forgiveness acknowledges the full extent of your hurt.

That's why forgiveness can't be rushed. Meaningful forgiveness occurs only after you have gotten through the shock and bewilderment of grief. It requires you to develop a realistic understanding of what has been lost. After all, you can't really forgive until you know *what* the offense is.

> A cry of *anguish* is heard in Ramah—weeping and *mourning* unrestrained. Rachel weeps for her children, refusing to be comforted—for they are dead. Matthew 2:18 (NLT)

Meaningful forgiveness also depends upon God's work in your heart. You need time to hear from God concerning your loss. You need time to pour out your heart to God, to know he understands your pain and your loss, and to receive comfort from him. You see, forgiveness doesn't require "head knowledge" that God wants you to forgive. Forgiveness requires "heart knowledge" that God knows your pain and that he will help you to forgive the offender.

If you are in an ongoing relationship with the person who has hurt you, you can express your grief to him. This is not the same as venting your anger. It is simply stating the offense and explaining why it was hurtful to you. Although painful to you both, this can be a very positive experience, because frequently the offender will know *that* you are hurt but have idea *why* it was hurtful. If you can control your anger, you can help the offender understand the nature of his/her offense.

Now, it is not always possible to express your grief to the offender, nor is it always advisable. The offender may be a stranger to you. Or the offense may have been a long time ago, you and the offender may now live in different cities, one or both of you may have remarried, or the offender may even be dead. In these cases, the **Empty Chair** technique can help you express your grief. Simply stand in front of an empty chair, imagine that the offender is in it, and express your grief to him/her, saying the things you have longed to say and that you have rehearsed in your mind a thousand times before.

> Inside I am like *bottled-up* wine, like new wineskins ready to burst. I must *speak* and find relief; I must open my lips and *reply*. Job 32:19-20 (NIV)

Talk out your grief to the empty chair. You may be surprised at the flood of things that come pouring out. Moreover, you may be surprised at the intensity of your grief. You will know when you are through, though, by the peace that God brings into your heart. When you are through, ask God to help you forgive the person, to give up your right to get even, and to finally let go of the hurt.

> And the *peace* of God, which *transcends* all understanding, will *guard* your hearts and your minds in Christ Jesus. Philippians 4:7 (NIV)

An alternative is the **Unmailed Letter**. Write a letter to the offender in which you spell out your pain, your sense of rejection, and your feelings of betrayal or of being abused. Write as long a letter or as short a letter as is necessary to express the full measure of your grief. At the end of your letter, write out a formal statement of forgiveness to the offender, identifying the offense and explaining the reason you are choosing to forgive him/her. When you have finished the letter, ask God to help you let go of the hurt and move on with your life.

➢ Relinquish your right to get even

Forgiveness is the choice not to strike back at the person who has hurt you. It is giving up your desire for revenge.

> You know that you have been taught, "An *eye* for an *eye* and a tooth for a tooth." Matthew 5:38 (CEV)

Revenge is a basic human instinct, but it is not a very effective way of living your life. Revenge can become an endless cycle of pain in an ever-widening circle of victims and offenders. In fact, revenge makes you a prisoner of your anger. Revenge prevents you from moving on with your life. That is why it is so important to choose forgiveness.

> If someone does wrong to you, do not *pay* him back by doing *wrong* to him. Romans 12:17 (NCV)

You may protest that it isn't fair to forgive the offender, letting him get off "scot-free." You're right; it's not fair. But fairness is a funny concept. It changes depending upon whether you are the victim or the offender. As the victim you demand justice. You want the offender punished immediately. But as the offender you seek mercy. You think of all the mitigating circumstances.

Forgiveness is a choice you make for your benefit, not the offender's. You choose to forgive others because of what it will do in your life in helping you heal and move on. You choose to forgive because Jesus has freely forgiven you, paying the penalty for your sins in his own body. You choose forgiveness because you trust God to work in the situation.

Furthermore, it is much better to let God settle the score than to try to do so yourself. Who do you think is better equipped to settle the score, you or God? You see, God is the only one who really knows the heart of a person, and he knows best how to deal with the offender.

> Never *avenge* yourselves. Leave that to *God*, for he has said that he will *repay* those who deserve it. Romans 12:19 (LB)

Remember that the unrepentant offender isn't really getting off "scot-free" anyway. The hurt and anger and sin in his life that led him to hurt you in the first place are extracting a high price from him. Those things are cruel taskmasters.

> When people *sin*, they earn what sin pays—*death*. Romans 6:23 (NCV)

Even if things aren't set right in this life, they will be in eternity. Everyone, great and small, rich and poor, good and evil, will stand before Jesus for judgment.

> (God) has set a *day* when the entire human race will be *judged* and everything set *right*. And he has already appointed the judge, confirming him before everyone by raising him from the dead. Acts 17:31 (Mes)

➢ Trust God for good fruit

When you choose to forgive someone who has hurt you, you give God a free hand to work in the situation. By letting go of the offense, you get out of God's way. That is why forgiveness is so powerful in any situation; it gives God a free hand.

Not only is God free to work in the life of the offender to bring judgment, he is also free to work in your life to bring good. No matter how bad a situation is, how deep the hurt, how great the injury, or how flagrant the wrong, God can use the situation as an opportunity to build good things into your life.

> We know that in *all things* God works for the *good* of those who love him. Romans 8:28 (NIV)

All means every situation, without exception. Sometimes it takes a bad situation to bring us back to God. Sometimes it takes a hopeless situation to teach us to trust God. Even in the worst of times, God can fill you with his love, build godly character in you, and set you free from your fears.

> That is why we never give up...our spirits are being *renewed* every day. For our present troubles...produce for us an immeasurably great *glory* that will last *forever!* 2 Corinthians 4:16-17 (NLT)

Your times of loss and pain often prepare you to help others in their times of pain. You see, the areas of your deepest hurt are often the areas in which you have the greatest insight, the greatest compassion, and the most to share. Moreover, you often have great faith for such situations, because you have seen how God brought you through your own crisis.

> He helps us in all our troubles, so that we are able to help *others* who have all kinds of troubles, using the *same* help that we ourselves have *received* from God. 2 Corinthians 1:4 (GN)

➢ Accept forgiveness as a process

Depending upon the severity of the offense against you and the extent of your injury from it, forgiving your offender may occur in stages. Forgiveness is not always a one-time event.

We know that grief occurs in waves, as your understanding and experience of the loss unfold. In the same way, you may need to choose to forgive your offender again and again, each time you come face to face with a new dimension of your loss. Serious offenses usually occur on many levels, and there may actually be multiple offenses bound up in the larger one.

Whenever the memory of the offense makes you angry or resentful, you need to acknowledge your grief, make a willful choice to forgive the offender, and release the matter into God's hands.

> Peter…asked, "Lord, *how often* should I forgive someone who sins against me? Seven times?" "No!" Jesus replied, "Seventy *times* seven!" Matthew 18:21-22 (NLT)

Jesus was saying that there is no limit on forgiveness. Seventy times seven is too many to count or to realistically keep track of. So, how often do you need to forgive the offender? As often as necessary. You need to continue to choose to forgive the offender until your anger and resentment go away.

Sometimes you may feel that the pain will never stop, that like peeling an onion you get through one level of forgiving and letting go only to discover another. But don't give up. You will get through it, and you won't always feel this way. Moreover, you should encourage yourself that your time isn't being wasted. God is building invaluable things into your life. Truly, it can be both the worst of times and the best of times for you.

Sometimes the memory of an offense brings pain without making you angry or resentful. When you are tormented by memories of an offense long after you have forgiven the offender, ask God to heal your memories.[5] God won't wipe your memory bank clean, but he will break the power of the memory to bring torment and emotional turmoil.

> He has sent me to bind up the brokenhearted, to proclaim *freedom* for the captives and *release* from *darkness* for the prisoners. Isaiah 61:1-2 (NIV)

Together with a close friend, pray that God will heal your memories and break their power over you. Then silently wait for God to bring a memory to your mind. You can simply say, "I have a memory." There is no need to describe the events in detail or even to name them. When you are ready, simply say, "Lord Jesus, I release this memory to you for healing."

Then your friend can pray for God's peace to come over the memory, for it to recede into holy forgetfulness, and for the emotional power of the memory to be broken forever. This process can be repeated as long as necessary. Conclude your time by thanking God that he cares for you and every detail in your life. Thank him that he came to set you free from the power of sin—both your own sins and the sins of others.

Rebuilding the Relationship

When you forgive someone, it does not mean that you must resume your relationship with them as if nothing happened. Restoring a relationship after an offense is a two-part transaction. The victim's part is forgiveness. But the offender's part is repentance and restitution. When the offense is serious, you should be reticent to resume the relationship until the offender has demonstrated changed behavior over time.

Likewise, when others forgive you for bad behavior, it does not automatically restore your relationship with them. You have to demonstrate your repentance to them, and you must work to rebuild the trust that you destroyed.

➤ The consequences of sin remain

Forgiveness releases the offender from the victim's anger and attempts at revenge. It gives God a free hand to work in the situation. But God doesn't ignore the offense, and he doesn't expect the victim to ignore it either.

> Don't be misled. Remember that you can't *ignore* God and get away with it. You will always *reap* what you *sow*! Galatians 6:7 (NLT)

Suppose your boss tells you to plant apple seeds, but you don't have any apple seeds and you don't want to go to the trouble to get them, so you plant pear seeds instead. What kind of tree will grow from your seeds? A pear tree, of course. Now when your insubordination becomes apparent, you may wish you had done differently and ask your boss to forgive you. If you are lucky, he will forgive you. Who knows? He may even let you keep your job. But do you think his forgiveness will change that pear tree into an apple tree? Not a chance.

In the same way, forgiveness does not remove the consequences of the offender's behavior. The damage remains and must be dealt with.

> Those who live only to satisfy their own sinful desires will *harvest* the *consequences* of decay and death. But those who live to please the Spirit will *harvest* everlasting life from the Spirit. Galatians 6:8 (NLT)

> ## The offender must truly repent

Defensiveness is the number one thing that will keep you from being able to repent. However, God says that discipline is a sign of his love, not his anger and hatred. If you can understand that God loves you even when you blow it, it will give you the confidence to listen and learn from the rebuke.

> Those whom I *love* I rebuke and *discipline*. So be *earnest*, and repent. Revelation 3:19 (NIV)

You see, the rebuke is directed against your behavior, not your self-worth. You are valuable to God because he created you and he loves you and he has good plans for you. Your worth as a person is never in question with God (no matter what messages you may have absorbed from others growing up). Therefore, in the rebuke, God is trying to correct your behavior, to show you a better way, and to teach you something that will make you happier and more effective for the rest of your life. He's not trying to smash you like a bug under his thumb.

> The Lord…is *patient* with you, because he does not want anyone to be *destroyed*, but wants all to turn away from their sins. 2 Peter 3:9 (GN)

It is absolutely essential that you listen to the rebuke and learn what your offense is. Many times you will have a vague sense that you have offended someone by their response to you, but you may have no real idea of the true nature of your offense. Moreover, a vague apology can be even more infuriating to the victim than no apology at all, because it seems to minimize the hurt and avoid personal responsibility.

> Not one of you has been *sorry* for your wickedness; not one of you has *asked*, "*What* have I done wrong?' Jeremiah 8:6 (GN)

Another thing that gets in the way of genuine repentance is thinking that your good intentions absolve you of responsibility for your actions. Your intentions are irrelevant to your responsibility for the offense, although they may be relevant to rebuilding the trust of your victim. True repentance offers no excuses or mitigating circumstances. It does not try to sugar coat what happened. It does not flinch from admitting that your behavior was absolutely wrong.

If they…repent…and say, "We have *sinned*, we have done *wrong*, we have acted *wickedly*." 1 Kings 8:47-48 (NIV)

Finally, true repentance identifies with the victim. It acknowledges the victim's pain, both the initial injury and the ongoing hardship. It recognizes the full extent of the damage caused by your behavior, even though it may be very painful for you to do so. You see, repentance is more concerned about the victim's pain than your own.

Let your *broken heart* show your *sorrow*; tearing your clothes is not enough. Joel 2:13 (GN)

The offender must take the initiative to make things right. At the very least, he must seek out the victim and offer his sincere apology. Then if he is wise, he will be silent. If the victim is not willing to forgive him, he must accept that he does not deserve forgiveness. If the victim is not willing to restore the relationship, he must abide by those wishes. But if the victim is willing to reach out to him, he should listen and learn because God will have something to teach him through the victim's perspective.

➢ The offender's behavior must change

Repentance is more than words. Your words mean nothing without a change in your behavior. The meaning of the word *repent* is to change direction, to turn around and go one-hundred-and-eighty-degrees in the opposite direction.

Prove by the way you live that you have really *turned* from your sins and turned to God. Matthew 3:8 (NLT)

First of all, if restitution is possible you must do everything you can to make the victim whole: financially, emotionally, and relationally.

But most importantly, you must demonstrate changed behavior that is ongoing. In other words, there has to be a one-hundred-and-eighty-degree change in your attitudes and your actions. That change must be ongoing. Doing the right thing once or twice is not enough; you have to make a permanent change in your lifestyle.

They should repent and turn to God and *prove* their repentance by their *deeds*. Acts 26:20 (NIV)

Relationships are built on trust over time. The greater the damage or betrayal, the longer it will take for the offender to rebuild the trust of the victim.

When others have repeatedly wronged you, God requires you to forgive them but he does not require you to trust them. He does not require you to instantly restore the relationship. To do so would be foolish.

Take for example, the wife of an abusive, alcoholic husband. His abuse of her and the children is ongoing until one day she finally kicks him out. A week later he returns, sober and remorseful, and asks her to take him back. Forgiving him and letting him move back in are entirely different issues. As a Christian, she must forgive him as soon as she has worked through her grief. However, she should not restore their relationship until he has proved to her that he can stay sober and control his temper. Moreover, she would be wise to enlist the aid to seasoned counselors to observe his behavior and help her judge his trustworthiness.

You see, neither the victim's forgiveness nor the offender's repentance automatically restores their relationship. Their relationship must be rebuilt over time, as the offender demonstrates changed behavior and the victim learns to trust him/her again.

Homework
Lesson #7: Healing Hurts through Forgiveness

Forgiveness Begins with God

1. Which statement in this section was the most helpful to you? Why?

2. Which of the scripture verses quoted in this section is your favorite? Why?

3. Do you keep score when you are wronged? Do you harbor resentment?

Forgiveness Is In Your Rational Self-Interest

4. Which statement in this section was the most helpful to you? Why?

5. Which of the scripture verses quoted in this section is your favorite? Why?

Working through Forgiveness

6. Which statement in this section was the most helpful to you? Why?

7. Which of the scripture verses quoted in this section is your favorite? Why?

8. When your behavior is corrected, do you feel your self-worth is attacked?

9. Ask your beloved. Are your apologies specific or vague?

Rebuilding the Relationship

10. Which statement in this section was the most helpful to you? Why?

11. Which of the scripture verses quoted in this section is your favorite? Why?

Special Assignment: Week 1 of 2

We do not allow you to write your own wedding vows. Your vows must be grounded in Biblical truth and church tradition. However, we encourage you to try to identify the particular values and priorities that will define your marriage.

12. For what purpose has God brought you together?

13. What are the ground rules by which you will live?

14. What are your goals for your marriage?

15. What are the personal commitments that you make to each other?

Begin your reflection by writing down your answers to these questions separately (two heads are always better than one). Then share your answers with one another. Work to develop a common statement (synthesis) of your vision for your marriage and your commitment to each other. Be as specific as you can in what you write. Avoid generalities that are so broad that they don't really mean anything.

Lesson #8: Speaking the Truth with Love

Love wants what is best for others. However, our thinking about what is best for them often gets a little fuzzy. You see, we tend to equate loving others with "being nice" to them, which means making them happy, giving them what they want, and avoiding any unpleasantness.

However, what if what they want is bad for them? What if they are hurting themselves or others? What if their behavior is counterproductive to their goals? What does love do then?

The Bible gives you a very simple guideline. Love always aligns itself with truth. Love doesn't ignore bad behavior in order to help others feel good about themselves. It doesn't ignore lies and self-deception in order to keep the peace. Love holds fast to the truth.

> *Love* is not happy with evil, but is *happy* with the *truth*. 1 Corinthians 13:6 (GN)

It is important to understand that what is best for others doesn't always make them happy. What they need to hear is not always what they want to hear. However, love gives others what they need instead of what they want. It is willing to risk unpleasantness in order to give them the truth.

In the Bible, love and truth are linked together. Both love and truth are intrinsic to God's nature and his character.

> But you, O Lord, are a merciful and gracious God, slow to get angry, full of unfailing *love* and *truth*. Psalm 86:15 (NLT)

Moreover, God's love and God's truth are both needed to save you. Love alone cannot save you; without truth you would not know your sin. Truth alone cannot save you, either, because without love you would never respond to God.

Surely his *salvation* is near to those who honor him…Unfailing *love* and *truth* have met together. Psalm 85:9-10 (NLT)

In God, love and truth meet. Together they reach out to you.

Lord, do not hold back your mercy from me; let your *love* and *truth* always protect me. Psalm 40:11 (NCV)

In the same way, you should reach out to others with both love and truth. In marriage, it is not enough to love one another. You must love each other with truth.

To my dear friend Gaius, whom I *love* in the *truth*, 3 John 1:1 (NIV)

Truth + Love = Transformation

➢ God's plan for you is transformation

Jesus didn't come so you could feel good about yourself the way you were. He wanted to set you free from your sins, every past hurt, all your fears, and every self-destructive behavior. God has good plans for you. He has a purpose for your life. God wants you to become everything he created you to be.

I urge you to live a life *worthy* of the *calling* you have received. Ephesians 4:1 (NIV)

In order for you to be everything God created you to be, you must deal with the residual habits of sin in your life. Bit by bit, the old habits and ways of thinking must be replaced with the new habits and new ways of thinking that enable you to fulfill God's purposes for your life.

You were taught to leave your old self—to stop living the evil way you lived before…you were taught to be *made new* in your hearts, to become a new person. That new person is made to be *like God*—made to be truly good and holy. Ephesians 4:22-24 (NCV)

What God has in mind is a thorough transformation of your thoughts, your emotions, your motives, your hopes, your dreams, and your habits.

> May God himself, the God of peace, *sanctify* you through and through. May your *whole* spirit, soul and body be kept *blameless* at the coming of our Lord Jesus Christ. 1 Thessalonians 5:23 (NIV)

However, God recognizes that you are not able to transform yourself, just as he recognized that you could never pay the penalty for your sins. Jesus not only paid the penalty for sin, he breaks the power of sin in your life. Transformation is possible because Jesus lives in you.

> For we are God's masterpiece. He has *created* us *anew* in Christ *Jesus*, so that we can do the good things he planned for us long ago. Ephesians 2:10 (NLT)

God is working in you. First, he puts the desire in your heart to do the right thing, and he gives you the willingness to obey him. Then God gives you the power to do what is right, and he gives you the ability to follow through. God's work in your heart and in your mind transforms you.

> For God is *working* in you, giving you the *desire* to obey him and the *power* to do what pleases him. Philippians 2:13 (NLT)

Lasting happiness and fulfillment come only when you allow God to transform you. Only then can you become all that God meant for you to be.

➤ Truth is essential for transformation

The only way you can be set free from your sins, your hurts, your fears, and your self-destructive behavior is to know the truth. However, simply knowing the truth is not enough. In order for the truth to set you free, you must apply it in your life. You must put it into practice.

> You are truly my disciples if you keep *obeying* my teachings. And you will *know* the truth, and the truth will set you *free*. John 8:31-32 (NLT)

When your practice falls short of the truth, when what you want is bad for you, when what you are doing is hurting yourself or hurting others, you need someone to speak the truth to you. You need someone to hold you accountable for your actions and to point out the damage you are doing. You need someone to challenge you to obey the truth and to show you how to bring your behavior back into line.

Speaking the truth can get ugly. It can cause pain, not only to the one being corrected, but also to the one offering the correction. But the pain that truth brings is necessary. In your body, you understand that pain is often part of medical treatment. Surgery or other procedures may be needed get rid of disease before healing and new growth can occur. In the same way, speaking truth can be painful as bad attitudes or bad behaviors are exposed. But if the correction is accepted, it will bring peace and spiritual growth to your life.

> It is never fun to be *corrected*. In fact, at the time it is always *painful*. But if we learn to obey by being corrected, we will do right and live at *peace*. Hebrews 12:11 (CEV)

Every one of us started out with a sinful nature. Even when we wanted to please God, we weren't able to do so. Jesus made restitution for our sins long ago, but leaving your sinful nature behind will be an ongoing process. It won't happen all at once. You will have to learn how to please God. And to do so, you'll need others to speak truth to you along the way.

> In the past you were full of *darkness*, but now you are full of *light* in the Lord. So live like children who belong to the light. Light brings every kind of goodness, right living, and *truth*. Try to learn what *pleases* the Lord. Ephesians 5:8-10 (NCV)

Sometimes the right thing to do isn't to keep the peace but to break it. Sometimes you need to cause conflict in order to address something that is wrong, that is bad for your spouse, or that is hurtful to others. Sometimes you need to help others recognize the truth about themselves. You need to call them out of darkness into the light.

➤ Truth transforms only when love is present

Truth has a hard side because it tells you something about yourself that you may not want to know. It asks something of you that requires you to put forth effort and exercise self-control. Therefore, you may not like truth very much when you hear it.

This hard side of truth is why truth alone cannot change you. Only truth spoken by those who love you can change you. Their love for you is what causes you to listen to their words and to try to understand the truth they share. Moreover, their love is what motivates you to change; it is what makes you want to respond to the truth.

> Speaking the truth with *love*, we will *grow up* in every way into Christ, who is the head. Ephesians 4:15 (NCV)

On the other hand, when you need to correct others, truth alone won't make you very effective. In fact, people who try to correct others without loving them first can be downright mean and judgmental. Truth becomes the billy club they use to beat people up with and to tear them down.

In contrast, when you love the people you need to correct, your love not only changes them, it changes you. It changes the way you present your message. It puts your focus on building others up, on meeting the underlying need that might have caused the problem in the first place, and on helping them repair the damage. Love seeks to build others up instead of tearing them down, even when they need correction.

> So when each separate part works as it should, the whole body *grows* and *builds itself up* through love. Ephesians 4:16 (GN)

In addition to transformation, truth spoken with love brings intimacy to relationships. In fact, the only way to move a relationship beyond the superficial is to speak the truth lovingly to each other. If you avoid saying the tough things, your relationship will never grow deeper. It will be as if you both are sipping tea, pretending not to see the elephant in the room. But if you are willing to confront the truth with love and support for each other, your relationship will grow stronger and more intimate.

> An *honest* answer is a sign of true *friendship*. Proverbs 24:26 (GN)

In the intimacy of marriage the truth you need to speak is not always correction. Sometimes you simply need to share your opinions and preferences with each other so that you can be on the same page as you move forward together. Such statements as "I don't like it when…I resent it when…I don't agree with you about…I don't see it that way…I think this is a problem…" can move you forward constructively when they are spoken with love.

> In the end, people appreciate *frankness* more than flattery. Proverbs 28:23 (LB)

When to Speak the Truth

Before you attempt to speak the truth to someone, you need to ask yourself these questions.

➢ What is my motive?

Always check your motive before you attempt to speak truth to someone. You need to ask yourself the question, "Why do I need to talk to this person about this issue?"

You see, sometimes the failure you notice in others is the failure you are struggling with yourself. If God is convicting you of pride, you will probably be very aware of others with big egos. If you are struggling with disorganization, you may be hypercritical of others who are disorganized.

Your criticism of others gives you the false sense of doing something about your failures or of distancing yourself from your shortcomings. However, criticizing others does nothing to change your own attitudes and behavior. It simply adds another shortcoming to the list: hypocrisy. Therefore, before you attempt to speak truth to someone, you need to ask yourself the question, "Is this message really meant for me?"

> How can you say to your *friend*, 'Let me take that little piece of dust out of your eye'? Look at yourself! You still have that big piece of wood *in your own eye*. You hypocrite! First, take the wood out of your own eye. Then you will see clearly to take the dust out of your friend's eye. Matthew 7:4-5 (NCV)

At other times, you may want to "speak truth" to others because they annoy you and you want to tell them off. Or, you may be angry with them and want to cut them down to size. Or, you may envy them and want to let them know that they aren't as perfect as they think they are. If so, you'd better hold your tongue. You won't be speaking as God speaks.

When God seeks to bring correction into your life, it is never for the purpose of tearing you down. God always brings correction in order to build you up and to make you stronger. Although he doesn't pull any punches about the truth, his words are loving and full of hope.

> My eyes will watch over them for their good...I will *build them up* and not tear them down. Jeremiah 24:6 (NIV)

In the same way, ask yourself, "Is my motive to build the person up?" If it isn't, then you are not speaking with love.

> For I want to use the authority the Lord has given me to *build you up*, not to tear you down. 2 Corinthians 13:10 (NLT)

The truth you speak must benefit the other person, not advance your own personal agenda. You intent must be to set people free from their problems, not to punish them. Your motive in speaking truth to others must be to strengthen them, to restore something that is broken in their lives, to support their spiritual growth, and to bring joy into their lives.

> We have been speaking in the sight of God as those in Christ; and *everything* we do, dear friends, is for your *strengthening*. 2 Corinthians 12:19 (NIV)

➤ Do I have the necessary relationship?

God hasn't called you to be the policeman of the world. Before you attempt to speak truth to someone, you need to ask yourself, "What kind of relationship do I have with him/her?"

> You can trust a *friend* who corrects you. Proverbs 27:6 (CEV)

No one has the right to bring correction into the life of a stranger. Without some sort of relationship, a stranger won't even listen to your words. But a friend will listen to your words because you have earned his/her trust. When you have proven your love for someone by your past actions, your relationship gives you the right to speak honestly with that person for his/her benefit.

However, your message must be in proportion to the relationship you have with the person. If you have a one-pound relationship, you can offer a one-pound correction. In contrast, if you have a ten-pound relationship, you can offer a ten-pound correction. But you should never offer a ten-pound rebuke to someone with whom you have only a one-pound relationship. Your relationship simply won't support it.

In casual friendships, you have a right to show your concern about something. You can say things like, "I am concerned because…" or, "Do you think that that was the best way…?" But your friend has no further obligation to you beyond listening to your concerns.

The deeper and more intimate your relationship, the more accountable you are to one another. In fact, in relationships in which you are accountable to one another (such as marriage) you are obligated to speak the truth to each other.

In addition, your message must be consistent with the area of authority you have in a person's life. Teachers have authority over the students in their classroom concerning academic subjects. Policemen have authority in the area of traffic and criminal law. Parents have authority over their children in their moral and social development as they train them for life.

> God is treating you as sons. For what *son* is not disciplined by his *father*? Hebrews 12:7 (NIV)

Correction is always a sign of relationship. In the examples of teachers and their students, policemen and the public, and parents and their children, correction is not only allowed, it is expected. In fact, the Bible says that if you try to have a relationship with God without accepting his correction, you are his illegitimate child!

> If God doesn't discipline you as he does all of his children, it means that you are *illegitimate* and are not really his children after all. Hebrews 12:8 (NLT)

➤ Am I willing to risk rejection?

It can be scary to speak the truth in love. When you have to say tough things to the people you love, you don't know how they will react. You don't know if their response to what you say will be positive or negative, whether they will end up loving or hating you, whether it will make matters between you better or worse.

> Am I now your *enemy*, just because I told you the *truth*? Galatians 4:16 (CEV)

No matter how lovingly you tell others the truth about themselves, they won't always respond very well. Particularly if it is something they don't want to hear, they may get offended and tell you it's none of your business. Others may become angry and hurl verbal insults at you. Some might even walk out of the room (or the house) in a huff.

> Correct a worthless bragger, and all you will get are *insults* and *injuries*. Proverbs 9:7 (CEV)

One of the biggest reasons that couples don't speak the truth with love to each other is that they are afraid of the possible consequences. They are afraid of being rejected. For that reason, they stuff their emotions, pretending that everything's OK, and drifting further and further apart from one another.

Love demands that you overcome that fear. Love requires you to speak the truth to those you love. Even though there is no guarantee that their response will be positive, you are obligated to try to reach them. Because of the love that God has put in your heart for them, you've got to be willing to risk their rejection in order to set things right.

> Now I am happy, but not because I hurt your *feelings*. It is because God *used* your hurt feelings to make you *turn back* to him. 2 Corinthians 7:9 (CEV)

➤ Is this the right time?

Timing is very important when you attempt to speak truth to someone you love. You need to choose a time and a place that enables the person to be receptive to your message. It is not fair to the person to bring up a sensitive matter when he/she is already physically tired, mentally exhausted, on a tight schedule, or preoccupied by something else. Nobody can give you a fair hearing under these circumstances, when his/her emotional reserves are so depleted.

> The *right* word at the *right* time is like precious gold set in silver. Proverbs 25:11 (CEV)

Love and truth can always wait for the right timing because their desire is to build others up, not to tear them down. If you find yourself bursting at the seams, unwilling to wait for a time when the person can be receptive to your message, you can be sure that you are not being motivated by love.

> A man has joy in an *apt* answer, and how delightful is a *timely* word! Proverbs 15:23 (NAS)

You need to allow sufficient time to discuss the matter. No one likes to be ambushed with the truth without proper time to respond. The more difficult your message, the more time a person will need to process what you say, to wrestle with the implications, and to sort out his/her feelings. Find a time when you have more than fifteen minutes to talk.

In addition, you need to find a private place to talk. Out of respect for the person, others should not be present when you discuss the matter. Privacy will avoid embarrassment, promote honesty between you, and build intimacy in your relationship.

> If your fellow believer sins against you, go and *tell* him in *private* what he did wrong. Matthew 18:15 (NCV)

How to Speak with Love

➢ Speak from God's point of view

Frequently it is something that irritates you about the other person that you first notice. That's OK, because it means that God is beginning to get your attention. However, your initial awareness is a signal to begin listening to God about a problem, not a license to speak to that person about it. The only way that you can speak the truth with love is to speak from God's point of view.

> Then speak as though *God* himself were *speaking* through you. 1 Peter 4:11 (NLT)

That is why you must not be impulsive. You must not rip off an e-mail or sound off your mouth. It takes time to clarify the message God wants you to speak. Invariably, you start by seeing the problem from your own point of view. You need to allow God to speak to your heart to show you the problem both from the other person's point of view and from God's point of view.

> The Spirit shows what is true and will come and *guide* you into the *full* truth. John 16:13 (CEV)

Seeing a problem from God's point of view is everything. It helps you identify the real issues and find lasting solutions. It helps you speak to the root problem and not just the symptoms.

> I speak the truth in Christ—I am not lying, my conscience *confirms* it in the *Holy Spirit*. Romans 9:1 (NIV)

One of the neat things about God is that he has hope, purpose, and vision for each of our lives, no matter how badly we may be messing up at the time. In order to speak truth to someone, you must have the same. You need to believe that there is something worthwhile in the person and to have vision for his/her life. Your heart must be filled with both love and hope for that person if you want to speak as God speaks.

For I know the *plans* I have for you," declares the Lord, "plans to prosper you and not to harm you, plans to give you *hope* and a *future*. Jeremiah 29:11 (NIV)

If you don't believe that a person can change, then you aren't the appropriate one to speak the truth to him. You need faith to speak the truth with love.

Frequently, your faith for a situation will come because you have experienced God doing a similar thing in your life or in the life of someone you know. At other times, God may simply speak quietly to your spirit, "Go for it," assuring you that he wants to work in the situation. No matter how it comes, you need the gift of faith if you want to be able to speak the truth with love.

But to each one is *given* the manifestation of the Spirit for the common good…to another *faith* by the same Spirit. 1 Corinthians 12:7-9 (NIV)

➢ **Affirm the person**

Affirmation is nothing more than putting your love into words. It is reminding others that they are valuable to you, that you remember and appreciate the good things they have done, and that you have confidence in them and vision for their future. Your words of affirmation bring comfort and encouragement to others.

It is particularly important to affirm others when you must say tough things to them. Your affirmation provides a context for the things you say. It lets them judge your motives and it clarifies your desire to help rather than hinder them. Words of affirmation set the tone of your discussion as one of encouragement rather than punishing disapproval.

When Paul wrote his first letter to the Corinthian church, he had to deal with some tough issues. The church was divided and quarreling, it was tolerant of sexual immorality, its worship was chaotic and unbecoming, and its theology on the resurrection was adrift. However, throughout his letter, Paul spoke words of affirmation. He didn't let the problems blind him to the good qualities of the Corinthian church.

I always *thank* God for you. 1 Corinthians 1:4 (NIV)

Paul begins his letter on a positive note. You see, if you are going to say tough things to someone, you need to affirm that you deeply love and care for him/her and that the relationship is important to you. Remember the good times, the things you share in common, and the accomplishments and qualities in him/her that you respect.

> Therefore you do not lack any *spiritual gift* as you *eagerly* wait for our Lord Jesus Christ to be revealed. 1 Corinthians 1:7 (NIV)

Express your confidence in him/her. When you are bringing correction into someone's life, that person needs to know that you have confidence in him/her to do the right thing and to make the necessary changes.

> He will keep you *strong* to the end, so that you will be *blameless* on the day of our Lord Jesus Christ. 1 Corinthians 1:8 (NIV)

In the midst of taking the Corinthian church to task for their divisions, Paul pauses to affirm his deep affection for them. It's as if he is saying, "I know these are tough words. I know this hurts, but I want you to know that my heart is big for you right now."

> I am not writing this to *shame* you, but to warn you, as my *dear children*. 1 Corinthians 4:14 (NIV)

Moreover, Paul pledges to send Timothy to help the Corinthians work through their problems. You see, when you speak truth to someone, you need to affirm that you will stand with them and help them make the necessary changes.

> That is the very reason I am *sending* Timothy—to *help* you do this…He will remind you of what I teach about Christ Jesus. 1 Corinthians 4:17 (NLT)

Well into Paul's letter, when it begins to sound as if the Corinthians have no redeeming qualities, Paul pauses again to praise them for their faithfulness in following his past instructions. Interestingly, this praise comes just before he gives them new instructions for restoring order to their worship. It's as if he is saying, "You've done it in the past. I know you can do it again."

> I praise you because you always *remember* me and *follow* the teachings that I have handed on to you. 1 Corinthians 11:2 (GN)

Finally, Paul ends his letter with an affirmation of his love.

My *love* to *all* of you in Christ Jesus. 1 Corinthians 16:24 (NIV)

As a practical matter, avoid using the word *but* as a conjunction between your affirmation and your correction. Using the word *but* tends to negate the affirmation in people's minds, as if it were mere window dressing. If you say, "Hey, you're a great person, *but*..." the emotional message most people hear is that you really don't think that they are all that great.

Try using the word *and* instead to link your affirmation with your correction. If you say, "We have a great marriage, *and* there're some issues we need to talk about," the emotional message that your spouse will hear is that you love your marriage and you want to keep it that way.

> You are so *rich* in all you have: in faith, speech, and knowledge, in your eager-
> ness to help and in your love for us. *And* so we want you to be *generous* also in
> this service of love. 2 Corinthians 8:7 (GN)

Consider these sentences from Paul's second letter to the Corinthians. With the conjunction *and,* it is an encouraging admonition drawing on their past successes. Were you to substitute the conjunction *but,* the emotional meaning would change completely. The implication would be that if they didn't come through with the giving, none of the other stuff would really matter. Use of the conjunction *but* would negate Paul's previous affirmation.

➤ Speak with humility

Humble people always get a better reception from others than prideful people do. If you want to create goodwill with others, approach them will a humble attitude. If you want your message to be humbly received, speak with humility.

> Be *humble* when you *correct* people who oppose you. Maybe God will lead
> them to turn to him and learn the truth. 2 Timothy 2:25 (CEV)

When you speak the truth to others, you should not approach them as one who is superior, as one having all the answers, or as a heavy-handed disciplinarian. Instead, approach them as one who is also fallible, who has also received correction and benefited from it, and who will doubtless receive correction in the future, also.

Brothers, if someone is caught in a sin, you who are spiritual should restore him gently. But *watch yourself,* or you also may be tempted. Galatians 6:1 (NIV)

Be meek and gracious in the way you introduce your topic. You may need to say things like this: "I may be totally wrong, but I'd like to talk with you about..." or "I may not have all the facts, but I'd really like to address this issue." Humility opens up the line for a productive discussion between you. In contrast, a know-it-all attitude can trap you in your own words.

Words from a wise man's mouth are *gracious,* but a fool is consumed by his own lips. Ecclesiastes 10:12 (NIV)

Part of humility is respecting the person's autonomy to make his/her own decision. God respects your autonomy by giving you free will. Shouldn't you show as much respect for others as God does? Therefore, the humble person asks, "Will you consider this?" instead of telling the person what to do. The humble person makes an appeal instead of giving an ultimatum.

I *appeal* to you, brothers, in the name of our Lord Jesus Christ, that all of you agree with one another so that there may be no divisions among you. 1 Corinthians 1:10 (NIV)

After you have spoken the truth to others, you may need give them time to digest what you've said and to consider the matter for themselves. Depending on their initial response, you may need to step back and give the Holy Spirit a chance to speak to their hearts. They must choose to change. You can't force them to do so.

➤ Be tactful

There is an old adage that you can catch more flies with honey than with vinegar. The same is true with people. Kind words are more effective than insults in getting your point across. If you want to be effective and persuasive in speaking the truth, you must be tactful. Use pleasant words.

The wise in heart will be called understanding, and *sweetness* of speech increases *persuasiveness.* Proverbs 16:21 (NAS)

For this reason, plan out ahead of time what you are going to say. Think through your approach to the subject matter. You see, the way you introduce the problem to the person and the way you frame the issues will largely determine whether he/she accepts or rejects your message. Therefore, be tactful in your approach to the problem.

Find a way to talk about the problem that isn't insulting and that doesn't put the person on the defensive. If you come home and say, "Hey, this place looks like a pigsty," you have started the conversation off on the wrong foot. But if you ask, "What do *we* need to do to have a more orderly home?" you are more likely to have a productive discussion.

> A *kind* answer *soothes* angry feelings, but harsh words stir them up. Proverbs 15:1 (CEV)

Remember that thoughtless, tactless words can cause deep emotional wounds, further damaging your relationship. But when you are careful in your choice of words and when you speak the truth tactfully, you can bring wholeness and healing to the person, thereby strengthening your relationship.

> *Careless* words *stab* like a sword, but *wise* words bring *healing*. Proverbs 12:18 (NCV)

Whenever you seek to speak truth to someone, be sensitive to their pain. Tactless words not only wound, they can crush a person's spirit, causing him/her to despair and give up hope.

> Kind words bring life, but *cruel* words *crush* your spirit. Proverbs 15:4 (GN)

You need to find a way to talk about the problem that is sensitive to the pain the person is feeling, whether from his own actions or the correction itself. Tactful words will help you be straight with him/her about the problem without increasing his/her pain unnecessarily.

Whatever the person's response to your message, be even-tempered. Mentally prepare yourself for a hostile or frosty reception so that you can continue to speak with tact. Don't match the person's emotions. Don't let his/her hostility trigger hostility in you.

A man of knowledge uses words with *restraint,* and a man of understanding is *even-tempered.* Proverbs 17:27 (NIV)

In an emotional situation, you need to maintain the patient and calm voice of reason. Continue to stay on target with your message; don't get distracted by side-issues or go off on a tangent. Keep your words tactful and your voice loving.

Correct, rebuke and encourage—with great *patience* and careful instruction. 2 Timothy 4:2 (NIV)

➢ Speak plainly

The more straightforward you are with others, the more forthcoming they will be with you. Transparency invites transparency, just as deception invites deception. When you speak plainly, you set a productive tone for your discussion with others.

I'm speaking as *plainly* as I can and with great *affection.* 2 Corinthians 6:13 (Mes)

When you seek to speak truth to others, you owe it to them to be specific. Don't speak in vague generalizations and don't sugar-coat the truth so much that your message is unintelligible. Don't be shy and beat around the bush; come right out and say what you mean.

By *setting forth* the truth *plainly* we commend ourselves to every man's conscience in the sight of God. 2 Corinthians 4:2 (NIV)

Give concrete examples that illustrate your point. Choose the most recent examples because people respond poorly to dredging up the past. First state the problem, as Paul did when he wrote the Corinthian church about their divisions.

My brothers, some from Chloe's household have informed me that there are *quarrels* among you. 1 Corinthians 1:11 (NIV)

Then explain what you mean by giving examples.

What I mean is this: *one of you says,* "I follow Paul"; another, "I follow Apollos"; another, "I follow Cephas"; still another, "I follow Christ." 1 Corinthians 1:12 (NIV)

➤ Pray during misunderstandings

No matter how careful you are with your words, sometimes people will misunderstand what you say. In fact, they may respond angrily to something that you never said at all. You may find yourself in a situation in which the lines of communication are incomprehensibly scrambled.

In these situations, prayer is the only way to unscramble your communication because Satan is the one who is scrambling the hearing of your words. The Bible says that Satan is in rebellion against God, that he hates the truth, that he is constitutionally unable to tell the truth, and that he is constantly spreading his lies around in your thoughts.

> *Everything* he says is a *lie*. Not only is he a liar himself, but he is also the *father* of all lies. John 8:44 (CEV)

Whenever you are weak or vulnerable, Satan shoots his lies at you like flaming arrows. Times of correction often become pitched battles in your heart and mind between truth and falsehood. Prayer is your indispensable weapon.

> In every battle you will need faith as your shield to stop the *fiery arrows* aimed at you by Satan. Ephesians 6:16 (NLT)

But if one of Satan's lies gets through and you unwittingly accept it as the truth, then you will be unable to understand the truth of God. It's as if your mind has been blinded and a veil put over your heart, so you cannot see the reality of the situation.

> *Satan*, the god of this evil world, has *blinded* the minds… 2 Corinthians 4:4 (NLT)

When this happens, you cannot talk or reason your way out of your predicament. More talk will only produce more words for Satan to scramble with his whispered lies. You must take the lying thoughts captive through prayer. You must expose the lies and replace them with the truth of Christ.

> We demolish arguments and every *pretension* that sets itself up against the knowledge of God, and we take *captive* every *thought* to make it obedient to Christ. 2 Corinthians 10:5 (NIV)

How should you pray when you need to unscramble the communication between you? Try praying Bible verses. Begin by praying for the person who is trying share the message. Pray that God would give him/her the right words to speak.

> Pray also for me, that whenever I open my mouth, *words may be given me* so that I will fearlessly make known the mystery of the gospel. Ephesians 6:19 (NIV)

Pray that he/she would be able to speak clearly.

> Please pray that I will make the message as *clear* as possible. Colossians 4:4 (CEV)

Then pray for the person who is receiving the message. Pray that Satan's lies would be exposed, and that he/she would have the faith to reject those lies.

> Take up the *shield* of faith, with which you can *extinguish* all the flaming arrows of the evil one. Ephesians 6:16 (NIV)

Pray for his/her mind to be opened to God's truth.

> I ask that your minds may be *opened* to see his light. Ephesians 1:18 (GN)

Pray that God would fill him/her with knowledge and understanding.

> We ask God to fill you with the *knowledge* of his will, with all the wisdom and *understanding* that his Spirit gives. Colossians 1:9 (GN)

Finally, pray for a spirit of unity so that you would not be fighting each other, but that together you would be able to find God's truth and his direction for the situation.

> May the God who gives endurance and encouragement give you a *spirit of unity* among yourselves as you follow Christ Jesus. Romans 15:5 (NIV)

Homework
Lesson #8: Speaking the Truth with Love

Truth + Love = Transformation

1. Which statement in this section was the most helpful to you? Why?

2. Which of the scripture verses quoted in this section is your favorite? Why?

3. Are you comfortable saying things people don't want to hear?

4. Ask your beloved. How do you respond to correction?

When to Speak the Truth

5. Which statement in this section was the most helpful to you? Why?

6. Which of the scripture verses quoted in this section is your favorite? Why?

7. How good are you at waiting for the right time to say something?

8. Ask your beloved. Have you corrected him/her in front of others?

How to Speak with Love

9. Which statement in this section was the most helpful to you? Why?

10. Which of the scripture verses quoted in this section is your favorite? Why?

11. Ask your beloved. Are you generous with words of affirmation?

12. Ask your beloved. When you talk, do you come across as a know-it-all?

13. Ask your beloved. How tactful are you in the way you say things?

14. Ask your beloved. Are you so vague that he/she often misses your point?

15. Have you and your beloved stopped to pray during an argument? What happened?

Special Assignment: Week 2 of 2

Last week you answered four questions about the purposes, goals, guidelines, and personal commitments that you wanted for your marriage. It is time to shape your thoughts into final form. Write for yourselves the "Oneness Covenant" that defines and personalizes the nature of the unity you hope to achieve in your marriage.

Write your covenant on the handout labeled "Oneness Covenant" (the font is BernhardMod BT if you want to duplicate it). This page will be added to your certificate of completion for the course. During the concluding ceremony, be prepared to affirm your covenant to your beloved.

Lesson #9: The Nature of Commitment

> ➤ **Making your marriage last**

As you approach marriage, your hearts are brimming with love for each other. You believe that you have found a lifetime love. And you have. But there is one thing you must understand. Love alone will not be able to sustain your marriage.

Life and love are like the waves of the sea. Sometimes they are at high tide, and sometimes they are at low tide. Sometimes there is turbulence, and sometimes there is calm. You will experience times that you are deeply and wondrously in love with each other; and you will experience times that you won't even like each other very much. Life is just like that.

> There is a time for everything, and a *season* for every activity under heaven.
> Ecclesiastes 3:1 (NIV)

And in those stressful times when your love is faltering, it is your commitment to marriage that will carry you through. It is your commitment to marriage that will keep you investing in your marriage until the love is easy again. It is your commitment that will keep you from writing off your marriage as a failed experiment. It is your commitment that will keep you from looking around for greener pastures.

You see, your marriage isn't in trouble just because you are struggling to love one another. Nor is your marriage in trouble because external circumstances or stress is pulling you in different directions. The only thing that can cause your marriage to be in trouble is when one or both of you abandon your commitment to your marriage. Your marriage can weather every other storm.

The traditional English wedding vow is a pledge…

> …to have and to hold from this day forward, for better for worse, for richer for poorer, in sickness and in health, to love and to cherish, till death us do part, according to God's holy ordinance; and thereto I plight thee my troth.[1]

It is a pledge to live together as husband and wife until one of you is taken in death. It is a promise not to abandon one another in difficult circumstances. It is a commitment to the other that has nothing to do with your emotions or personal fulfillment. It simply declares, "Come what may, I will be here with you and we will face life together."

You may have been curious about the final words of the vow, that Middle English phrase "thereto I plight thee my troth." Translated, it means, "I pledge my faithfulness to you." I am making a solemn promise, and I will keep my word. My personal integrity and reputation are on the line. I am committed to you.

There is no profound secret to making your marriage last. It is simply a matter of standing by your commitment, of honoring your wedding vow. Sometimes it is simply a matter of "hanging in there" until you can see the light at the end of the tunnel.

➢ Cherishing your spouse

But the wedding vow also promises "to love and to cherish." You see, being committed to each other doesn't mean that you resign yourself to a loveless marriage. Quite the contrary. It means that you are committed to loving your spouse regardless of the circumstances. It means that you will continue to act in love toward your spouse whether the feelings are there are not.

We end this course as we began: love is a choice. Love is defined by the way you think, the actions you take, the priorities you choose. Love isn't driven by feelings, although feelings inevitably follow. It's just that feelings aren't in the driver's seat of your relationship. Love is.

This is the irony of marriage: although your love for one another caused you to marry, henceforth, your marriage will cause you to love one another. You see, when your love begins to falter, it is your marriage that will keep love alive. Because of your commitment to your marriage, you will continue to invest in your spouse, you will continue to act in loving ways toward him/her, you will continue to put his/her interests above your own, and you will reach out through your hurt and confusion and anger to affirm your unity in calling and purpose.

> Husbands, *love* your *wives*, just as Christ loved the church and gave himself up for her. Ephesians 5:25 (NIV)

After you are married, the issue of whether you have a common calling and purpose no longer exists. You do, simply by the fact that you are married to each other. God has joined you together. By definition you have a common calling and purpose.

For this reason, you should agree that after your wedding, you will never let the word "divorce" escape your lips. Never wonder whether you should be married to each other. Your marriage is a done deal. And God wants it to last as long as you both are alive.

> So they are no longer two, but one. Therefore what *God* has *joined* together, let man not separate. Matthew 19:6 (NIV)

Instead, you should invest your energies in discovering the calling and purpose God has for your marriage. After you are married, it is easy to get lazy and stop nurturing your relationship. It is easy to take your marriage for granted. But if you do so, you will not be cherishing one another.

You see, to cherish your spouse means to remain active in the cultivation of your love. It means proactively doing things to nurture your relationship. It means marking the milestones of your life together and celebrating your accomplishments.

> For this reason I remind you to *kindle afresh* the gift of God which is in you. Timothy 1:6 (NAS)

In marriage you are receiving a marvelous gift from God. But gifts from God are never static; they are always dynamic. The Apostle Paul compares the gifts of God to fire. A blazing fire inevitably burns down to embers. And if you want the fire to continue to burn, you must continue to stir up the embers and add more fuel.

➤ Nurturing your whole marriage

As we have seen, your marriage is a multifaceted relationship, and to remain healthy it must function on many levels. God gave you a spirit, a soul, and a body when he formed you in your mother's womb. And he intends that in marriage your spirits, your souls, and your bodies be joined together in unity.

> May your *whole spirit, soul and body* be kept blameless at the coming of our Lord Jesus Christ. 1 Thessalonians 5:23 (NIV)

It is not unlike a car with four wheels. If one tire gets a flat, you can continue to drive the car but the ride won't be the same. Similarly, if one area of your relationship goes flat, it doesn't change the fact that you are married, but you are both in for a bumpy ride.

For this reason many couples find it helpful to have a weekly Marriage Staff Meeting,[1] a concept developed by David & Teresa Ferguson. The idea is to set aside a time with your spouse to discuss each area of your marriage. By ensuring that no area is overlooked, the meetings strengthen your marriage and ensure that no area "goes flat."

However, the chief benefit of the Marriage Staff Meeting lies in the reflective nature of your discussion with one another. Much of the dialog in marriage is simply the factual exchange of information. "I have a meeting tomorrow at 8:00 a.m. Sally made an A on her test. The garbage disposal is broken. Do you want to renew this magazine subscription?" Such dialog is necessary, but it does not nurture your marriage.

The purpose of the Marriage Staff Meeting is to step back from the immediacy of your daily lives and look at the trends. What seems to be happening in this pattern of events? What is God saying to us? What are the underlying problems that are causing this situation? How have things changed in this area over the past few months? Where do we need to go from here? How have we overcome similar problems in the past? These are the kinds of questions that allow you to develop unity and intimacy in your marriage.

The guidelines for holding a Marriage Staff Meeting are simple: do what works for you. Schedule a time that works in your schedule. Any time is fine as long as you each can be relaxed and reflective. Find a place that works for you. It just needs to be a place that is quiet, without interruptions or distractions, where you can have a quality discussion with each other. If one place doesn't work out, try somewhere else next week. Some of you will be stimulated by a variety of locations, and others will enjoy the intimacy of having that one special place.

Whatever you do, the Marriage Staff Meeting ought to feel like a secret rendezvous with your beloved. You should look forward to it with anticipation because of the intimacy it brings to your marriage. It is a chance to get away—just the two of you—from all of your responsibilities and distractions, to cherish each other, and to nurture your marriage.

Develop an agenda that works for you. Your goal is to discuss every area of your marriage. Use names or categories that make sense to you. Just be sure that you have a category for every area of your marriage: spirit, soul, body, responsibilities. Then organize the categories in a sequence that facilitates your discussion. Choose a beginning topic that helps you break the ice and open up to each other. Choose an ending topic that leaves you with a sense of intimacy with your spouse.

Sample Agenda: Family Staff Meeting

1. Schedule. What is coming up in the next week or month? Are you excited or happy? Are you worried or anxious?

2. Budget. Where do we stand financially? What large expenses lie ahead? What are our financial goals?

3. Children. What is going on with our kids? How should we respond?

4. Health. What is going on in your body? What about your sleep, diet, exercise, or illness?

5. Sex. How are you feeling about this area? What would increase your satisfaction?

6. Spiritual. What are you reading in the Bible? What does God seem to be saying to you?

7. Emotional. How are you feeling about your life? What are your hopes and dreams?

Pastoral Counseling Session

A Personal Relationship with God

➢ Transformational power

The most important decision you will ever make is to establish a personal relationship with God. You see, you can't live a successful Christian life by your own effort, by willing yourself to do the right thing. It is not humanly possible!

> For God is *working* in you, giving you the desire to obey him and the *power* to do what pleases him. Philippians 2:13 (NLT)

The only possible way to live a life that is pleasing to God—to do the things God has called you to do, to be the person God created you to be, to experience success in your marriage or your relationships with others—is to have God's power and his thoughts dwelling in you.

> I pray that from his glorious, unlimited resources he will give you mighty *inner* strength through his Holy Spirit. And I pray that Christ will be more and more at *home* in your hearts as you *trust* in him. Ephesians 3:16-17 (NLT)

When you put your trust in Jesus, the God of the Universe, the Savior of the World comes to live in your heart. Wow. Through the Holy Spirit, he speaks to your spirit, changing your thoughts and your desires, and transforming you from the inside out.

Getting to know Jesus is like any other personal relationship. The more you focus your attention on him, the more you listen to what he says, the more sensitive you become to his guiding, the more at home he will be in your heart. You see, trusting Jesus is an ongoing process. Day by day, moment by moment, you must commit your situation to him and listen for his prompting.

> Once the Spirit of him who raised Christ Jesus from the dead lives *within* you he will, by the same Spirit, bring to your whole being new *strength* and *vitality*. Romans 8:11 (JBP)

The mark of Jesus making his home in you is a heart overflowing with joy and peace and hope. Most people think that the joy and peace and hope you feel depends upon your circumstances. When things are going well, you feel happy. When things are going badly, you feel deflated. But God has a better way.

Joy and peace and hope are gifts of God, the fruit of the Holy Spirit, that come from having the power of God at work in your inner being. They are your spiritual birthright, regardless of your circumstances.

> May the God of hope fill you with all *joy* and *peace* as you trust in him, so that you may overflow with *hope* by the power of the Holy Spirit. Romans 15:13 (NIV)

Sometimes when you put your trust in Jesus, he will smooth out your circumstances. He will work out situations or timing or relationships in a way that you yourself couldn't.

But other times when you put your trust in Jesus, he will seek to change you instead of your circumstances. You see, God wants to transform your inner being to be just like Jesus. Even though your circumstances are unchanged, you can still experience God's joy and peace and hope. It may defy all human logic, but the power of God working in you can give you peace and shape your thoughts.

> And the peace of God, which surpasses all comprehension, will *guard* your *hearts* and your *minds* in Christ Jesus. Philippians 4:7 (NAS)

➤ Forgiveness of sins

Now the one thing that will prevent Jesus from making his home in your heart is sin—*your* sin. You see, sin and God are polar opposites; they cannot coexist.

> The sinful mind is *hostile* to God. It does not *submit* to God's law, nor can it do so. Romans 8:7 (NIV)

Deep down you probably know that you haven't measured up to what God requires of you. Moreover, your conscience stands as a witness against you, accusing you whenever you do something wrong. The experience of guilt and shame is universal to the human condition.

They demonstrate that God's law is written within them, for their own *consciences* either *accuse* them or tell them they are doing what is right. Romans 2:15 (NLT)

Even when people reject God's standards, they still can't live up to the (relaxed) standards they set for themselves. You see, the inability to do what you know is right is the fundamental aspect of your sinful nature.

In my *sinful* nature…I have the *desire* to do what is good, but I *cannot* carry it out. Romans 7:18 (NIV)

Fortunately, God's love for you is greater than his hatred of sin. The life, death, and resurrection of Jesus have made it possible for you to be reconciled to God.

For God was in *Christ, reconciling* the world to himself. 2 Corinthians 5:19 (NLT)

When Jesus died on the cross, his blood paid the penalty for your sin and purchased your freedom. No longer does sin have to separate you from God because Jesus' blood makes it possible for your sins to be forgiven.

For God in all his fullness was pleased to live in Christ, and by him God *reconciled* everything to himself. He made *peace* with everything in heaven and on earth by means of his *blood* on the cross. Colossians 1:19-20 (NLT)

Moreover, the resurrection of Jesus broke the power of sin and death in the world. No longer do you have to be captive to your sinful nature. Jesus makes it possible for you to enjoy the blessings of his kingdom when he dwells in your heart.

God has freed us from the *power* of darkness, and he brought us into the *kingdom* of his dear Son. The Son paid for our sins, and in him we have *forgiveness*. Colossians 1:13-14 (NCV)

Jesus has already done the heavy lifting, but what does God require of *you* in order for you to be reconciled to him? Simply your *faith* in Jesus.

You were saved *by faith* in God…This is God's *gift* to you, and not anything you have done on your own. Ephesians 2:8 (CEV)

First of all, you need to put your trust in Jesus. This is more that simply believing the truth about him, though that is necessary. Saving faith is trusting yourself to Jesus, putting yourself in his hands and trusting him to take care of you.

Secondly, you must repent of your sins. You need to clearly and specifically own up to what you have done wrong, and ask God to forgive you. You must be sincere in your repentance, taking steps to change your future behavior with God's help. However, you can approach God with confidence that he wants you to be reconciled with him. You see, God will always forgive your sins whenever you come to him with a repentant heart.

> But if we *confess* our sins to God, he can *always* be trusted to *forgive* us and take our sins away. 1 John 1:9 (CEV)

➢ Dying to sin

When you receive forgiveness for your sins and enter into a personal relationship with Jesus, your spiritual citizenship changes. You are born into God's kingdom. You are adopted into God's family. And you will live with God forever, first in this world as Jesus dwells in your heart, and later on in heaven with him for all eternity.

> Then our Lord and Savior Jesus Christ will give you a glorious welcome into his *kingdom* that will last *forever*. 2 Peter 1:11 (CEV)

Just like that, your spiritual citizenship ceases to be in the kingdom of darkness. Sin no longer owns you. Satan no longer has authority over you. You belong to God, and your highest purpose is to give praise to God through your words and your actions.

> But you are a *chosen* people, a royal priesthood, a holy nation, a people belonging to God, that you may declare the *praises* of him who called you out of *darkness* into his wonderful light. 1 Peter 2:9 (NIV)

Baptism is the public acknowledgement that you have changed kingdoms. When you go under the water it is like a burial of your sinful nature. You are renouncing the kingdom of darkness. When you come up out of the water it is like a spiritual resurrection. You are embracing your new life in the kingdom of God.

If it's an *initiation* ritual you're after, you've already been through it by sub-mitting to *baptism*. Going under the water was a *burial* of your old life; com-ing up out of it was a *resurrection*, God raising you from the dead as he did Christ. Colossians 2:12 (Mes)

Even though sin no longer has the power of life and death over you, sin is still active in this world. Satan will continue to lie, tempt, and deceive, trying to trick you back into the ways of sin and darkness. In order to resist temptation, you must learn to think of the sinful part of your life as dead and in the past, replaced by an infinitely more satisfying life done God's way.

> *Consider* yourselves to be *dead* to sin, but *alive* to God in Christ Jesus. There-fore do not let sin reign in your mortal body so that you obey its lusts. Romans 6:11-12 (NAS)

In its stead, you should actively embrace everything God has for you. Read the Bible to try to get to know God better. Practice giving God your full attention so that you can learn to recognize his voice. Get together with other Christians for instruction and encouragement. Allow God to change the way you think and the way you respond in difficult situations.

> Offer yourselves as a *living* sacrifice to God, *dedicated* to his service and pleas-ing to him. Romans 12:1 (GN)

As a Christian, you can expect God to hold you to a higher standard. Certain things you were used to doing before your new life in Jesus may no longer be appropriate. But God isn't being mean when he calls you to live up to a higher standard. He isn't trying to keep you from having fun. Not at all! He's trying to keep you from getting hurt. Sinful behavior may seem promising at the begin-ning, but it always leads to negative consequences: to pain, to loss, to spiritual death.

> Don't copy the behavior and customs of this world, but let God *transform* you into a new person by changing the way you *think*. Romans 12:2 (NLT)

Satan wants you to believe that sin makes you happy; in reality, sin always ends up bringing you grief. He makes sinful actions seem like the ultimate free-dom and abandon; in reality, they bring entanglement and long term conse-quences.

The happiest and freest people in the world are those who are least entangled in sin. That is why you must be ruthless toward the sin in your life. You cannot afford to indulge it, to tolerate it, to overlook it. Sin is like a poison-pill in your life. You have to get rid of it.

> Those who belong to Christ Jesus have *nailed* the passions and desires of their sinful nature to his *cross* and crucified them there. Galatians 5:24 (NLT)

The Marriage Bed

➤ Sexual sin

Over the past forty years the sexual mores of our culture have been turned upside down. Behavior that was once considered shameful has come out into the open as accepted practice. Approximately 50% of marrying couples live together before they marry.[1] TV shows and movies portray unmarried sex for young adults as normative. Homosexuality is now vying for the respectability (and benefits) of marriage.

Although our culture has changed, God has not changed. Nor have the needs of human beings changed. God still prohibits sin because it is destructive to the people involved.

> Do not be deceived: Neither the *sexually immoral* nor idolaters nor adulterers nor male prostitutes nor homosexual offenders…will inherit the *kingdom* of God. 1 Corinthians 6:9-10 (NIV)

Sexual sins always figure prominently in any list of prohibited behavior. That is because sexual sins cause you to sin against your own body, against the purpose for which God created your sexuality.

> In sexual sin we *violate* the *sacredness* of our own bodies, these bodies that were made…for "becoming one" with another. 1 Corinthians 6:18 (Mes)

You see, God created your sexuality for one purpose and one purpose only: to build the marriage bond between husband and wife.

> The marriage bed is to be *undefiled*; for *fornicators* and *adulterers* God will judge. Hebrews 13:4 (NAS)

"Fornicators" is a quaint old word for people who have sex without being married. The fall of this word into disuse is an indication of just how much our sexual mores have changed. Premarital sex defiles the marriage bed because it brings into marriage the burden and history of sexual sin. That which God intended to be holy is cheapened in your own eyes.

In this regard it doesn't matter whether you were in a "committed relationship" or had a one night stand. It doesn't matter whether you were engaged to marry your sexual partner or moved in together because one of you lost your job. As the saying goes, what part of "Thou Shalt Not" do you not understand? Sexual intercourse isn't your right until after you are married, until the ring is on your finger and your commitment to each other is legally binding.

Adulterers are married people who have sex outside of their marriage. Extramarital sex defiles the marriage bed by breaking your marriage vow of sexual purity and faithfulness to your spouse. It is a body blow against your marriage. It is the most fundamental betrayal.

Sexual sin always leads to negative outcomes. You can't defile your body without unintended consequences. Researchers have found that cohabitating women experience five times as much depression as married women.[2] They are twice as likely to believe that their relationships are in trouble.[3] They are also eight times more likely to cheat on their partner than married women are.[4] In addition, cohabitating men cheat four times as much as married men do.[5]

Cohabiting couples are twice as likely to experience domestic violence as married couples.[6] Moreover, it is five times more likely that the violence will become "severe"[7] and nine times more likely that the violence will end in death.[8] If that were not enough, the poverty rate for children living in cohabiting homes is five times the poverty rate for children living in married homes (31% vs. 6%).[9]

The negative outcomes continue even after you marry your beloved. Cohabitation teaches you a commitment to one another that is conditional. It ingrains in your psyche a fear that intimate relationships are fragile and transitory. Moreover, it impairs your social skills. Spouses who lived together before marriage interact with each other less than spouses who did not cohabit.[10] They offer each other less support and demonstrate more negative and less positive problem solving.[11]

Spouses who cohabited experience more problems with drug and alcohol abuse in their marriages than spouses who did not.[12] Adultery is more common,[13] as are problems with a spouse who is too independent.[14] Married couples who lived together before they married are 80% more likely to separate[15] and 46% more likely to divorce that married couples who did not cohabit.[16]

> But there must be no *sexual sin* among you, or any kind of evil or greed. Those things are not *right* for God's holy people. Ephesians 5:3 (NCV)

God prohibits sexual sin because it is destructive to you and it is destructive to your marriage. It has no place in God's plan for you.

➤ Self-control

Some of you are feeling pretty good about now. You are encouraged in your decision to remain chaste until marriage, and you are looking forward to its benefits. You need to know that God will richly reward your obedience to him.

Others of you don't like talking about this subject. You bristle at the moral condemnation of living together before marriage. You resent the notion that it makes any difference *when* you start having sex as long as you're getting married anyway.

What you must understand is that it makes a difference to God.

> God wants you to be *holy* and to stay away from sexual sins. He wants each of you to learn to *control* your own *body* in a way that is holy and honorable. 1 Thessalonians 4:3-4 (CEV)

You see, God has good plans for you. He has more vision for you than you do for yourself. He wants you to be able to enjoy every good thing that he has prepared for you. But he also knows that self-control is absolutely essential to success in every area of life.

No athlete can compete and win without training, and all athletic training requires discipline and sacrifice and self-control. It requires making yourself do something that you don't always want to do in order to achieve your goal.

> All athletes practice strict *self-control*. They do it to win a *prize* that will fade away, but we do it for an eternal prize. 1 Corinthians 9:25 (NLT)

Nothing worthwhile is achieved without sacrifice and self-control. School requires study and homework. Jobs require dependability, cooperation, and intelligent effort. Staying healthy requires washing your hands, eating the right foods, physical exercise, and adequate sleep.

You should not expect it to be any different for marriage. God designed marriage to work in a certain way, and you must respect the constraints of his design.

God designed sexual intercourse solely for marriage and the courtship period for developing sexual self-control.

You're going to need sexual self-control in marriage: for remaining faithful to your spouse, for showing consideration of each other's needs, for pregnancy and illness and business trips. You'll need self-control in every other area, too. Marriage is the social and economic workhorse of society, and as husband and wife you will assume many responsibilities for yourselves and for others.

Without self-control you will destroy the very thing that you are working for, that you most desire. You see, temptation is part of life. There is always the tension between doing the right thing and doing the easy thing. As an athlete, do you get up to run or do you stay in bed? As a student, do you do your homework or do you go out with friends? Concerning your health, do you pack a nutritious lunch or do you grab something at the vending machine? Meeting goals always involves making hard choices.

> We are *tempted* by our own *desires* that drag us off and trap us. Our desires make us sin, and when sin is finished with us, it leaves us *dead.* James 1:14-15 (CEV)

As an engaged couple your goal is a successful marriage, including a fulfilling sexual relationship. You will have to make some hard choices in order to obtain your goal. Do you choose to indulge your sexual desire in the present? Or do you delay sexual gratification, developing self-control and a clear conscience, in order to have the very best marriage you can possibly have? You can't have it both ways. In life there is always the trade-off between present pain and future gain.

> No *discipline* seems pleasant at the time, but *painful.* Later on, however, it produces a *harvest* of righteousness and peace for those who have been trained by it. Hebrews 12:11 (NIV)

Fortunately, God doesn't expect you to deal with your temptations alone. He stands ready to help you. In fact, there is no temptation that God can't help you beat. In this way, he is like a trusted athletic coach.

> You are *tempted* in the same way that everyone else is tempted. But God can be *trusted* not to let you be tempted too much, and he will show you how to *escape* from your temptations. 1 Corinthians 10:13 (CEV)

The first way God helps you overcome a temptation is to expose it for what it really is. No sin is nearly so attractive or beguiling when viewed simultaneously with its negative consequences. Satan doesn't believe in truth in advertising, but God does. Sin always brings some sort of death with it.

A second way God helps you overcome a temptation is to give you a strategy for avoiding situations in which you are likely to be tempted. For example, if you struggle with drunkenness, don't go to bars. If you are an unmarried couple, don't spend the night together. It's just common sense.

A third way God helps you overcome temptation is to give you a new focus for your thoughts. You see, your thoughts drive your behavior. To beat your temptation you need to stop dreaming about it, and you need to think about something else instead. Think about your new life in Christ. Memorize Bible verses. Learn to serve others. Occupy yourself with the things that please the Lord.

> You have been raised to life with Christ, so *set your hearts* on the things that are in heaven, where Christ sits on his throne at the right side of God. Colossians 3:1 (GN)

Homework
Pastoral Counseling Session

A Personal Relationship with God

1. Which statement in this section was the most helpful to you? Why?

2. Which of the scripture verses quoted in this section is your favorite? Why?

3. Do you have a personal relationship with God? Please explain.

The Marriage Bed

4. Which statement in this section was the most helpful to you? Why?

5. Which of the scripture verses quoted in this section is your favorite? Why?

6. Has your marriage bed been defiled? Please explain.

About The Use of Scripture

Using Scripture

➤ The power of scripture

The Bible is God's gift to you. It allows you to know him, to learn his ways, and to be reconciled with him.

> Since you were a child you have known the Holy Scriptures which are able to make you wise. And that wisdom leads to salvation through faith in Christ Jesus. 2 Timothy 3:15 (NCV)

The Bible is God's living word to you. In its pages you will find instruction, correction, hope, and encouragement according to your present need.

> All Scripture is God-breathed and is useful for teaching, rebuking, correcting and training in righteousness, so that the man of God may be thoroughly equipped for every good work. 2 Timothy 3:16-17 (NIV)

As you are exposed to the words of God in the Bible, you will be changed. The way you think about things will change. The desires of your heart will change. The things you do and how you choose to spend your time will change. You see, God is ALIVE and he is active in the world today—that's the whole point of Jesus' resurrection.

> For the word of God is living and active. Sharper than any double-edged sword, it penetrates even to dividing soul and spirit, joints and marrow; it judges the thoughts and attitudes of the heart. Hebrews 4:12 (NIV)

For this reason, you are encouraged to search the scriptures for yourself. Where a single scripture or a part of a scripture is quoted in the text, you may want to read the entire passage or chapter. In virtually every instance, the underlying passage is wonderfully rich and full of meaning and encouragement. Reading the passage for yourself will increase your knowledge of God and stir up your faith; and there is no better way to begin your marriage together.

➢ Guidelines for quoting scripture

In this book, quoted scriptures have been chosen with great care and respect—for God and for you.

First of all, scriptures have not been quoted **out of context**. The meaning ascribed to a quoted verse will be consistent with the meaning of the whole chapter or passage. At times, a verse has been quoted because it expresses a general Biblical principle. The particular application made in the text may differ from the situation to which it is applied in the chapter or passage; however the general principle will be unchanged. Furthermore, idiomatic translations are quoted only when they convey an idea with particular clarity or emotional impact. They are never quoted when they introduce a meaning unsupported by the careful reading of a word for word translation.

Secondly, scriptures have been quoted in a manner that reflects the **whole counsel** of the Bible. It is possible to find passages in scripture that at first glance appear to contradict one another. However, we know that God as the All-Knowing author of Truth would never contradict himself. Therefore, it is necessary to look at the scriptures together to see the "big picture" and to clarify what God is saying—and just as importantly, what he is *not* saying. You see, God's truth is not an Either/Or proposition in which we must choose between competing extremes. It is a Both/And proposition in which we find a mature balance that speaks to the diversity of human experience. Therefore, scripture has been quoted in a manner that is consistent with the broad themes of the Bible.

Translating Scripture

➢ Difficulties faced by translators

Today, we are blessed with a variety of Bible translations, and each is useful, provided you understand the purpose of the translators. As you may know, the Old Testament was written in Hebrew, the language of the children of Israel. The New Testament was written in Greek, the trade language of the Middle East during the time of the Roman empire.

The first challenge of translation is differences in the **grammatical structure** of the languages. English sentences arrange nouns, verbs, adjectives and adverbs differently from either Hebrew or Greek sentences.

The second challenge of translation is **idiomatic expressions**, such as figures of speech. Groups of words often mean something very different from the literal translation of the words.

A third challenge of translation is the **cultural context**. Egypt at the time of the Pharaohs, Israel at the time of the Romans, and America in the twenty-first century are very different places. The physical geography, political climate, economic realities, social customs, and religious frames of reference are different. Standards of beauty, foods commonly eaten, methods of home construction, and modes of travel are different. Therefore, an object or event may once have had a profound or emotionally charged meaning that is totally lost on us today.

The fourth challenge of translation is the **mystery of God**. Sometimes the text itself is ambiguous. Perhaps we simply lack spiritual understanding in an area. Or perhaps it is something unknowable this side of heaven. In any case, those things about God which remain a mystery to us are an opportunity for us to trust his wisdom and his goodness.

➢ Types of translations

Bible translators choose different strategies to deal with these difficulties.

The **Word for Word** translators seek a translation that conforms as closely as possible to the original text, accepting a certain amount of grammatical awkwardness as a tradeoff. Their goal is to add nothing to their translation that is not in the original text. These make good study Bibles because it is fairly easy to trace a word back to its original Hebrew or Greek. However, considerable background study may be necessary to understand the cultural context.

The **Thought for Thought** translators aim for a text that reflects contemporary English usage. Their goal is readability, with a grammar and word usage that makes it accessible to its audience. Although the word usage does substitute contemporary equivalents for culturally archaic words, the intent is to produce a fairly spare translation that adds nothing theologically that is not in the original text. These are good Bibles for general reading.

The **Paraphrase** translators have more of a devotional purpose in mind. Their goal is for their readers to understand what they are reading. As such, they seek to spell out theological concepts and to express scriptural truths in current idioms. However, in the attempt to make the text clear to their readers, they often insert a particular theological point of view when the original text is not nearly so specific. At their best, their emotional impact is unsurpassed. At their worst, they can be misleading. Again, they are useful, but before you run with a concept you get from one of these translations, you need to check a study Bible first.

The following table places ten commonly-used translations on a continuum from the most literal Word for Word translation to the most idiomatic Paraphrase.

Word for Word	Thought for Thought	Paraphrase

New American Standard — King James Version — New International Version — New Century Version — New Living Translation — Good News Translation — Contemporary English Version — Living Bible — JB Phillips Translation — The Message

> **Available English translations**

Ten of the more common translations have been quoted in this book.

New American Standard (NAS): Published in 1971and updated in 1995 by the Lockman Foundation, it has a reading level of Grade 11. Scholars worked to produce a literal translation "as close as possible to the actual wording and grammatical structure of the original writers." The NAS is a good study Bible.

King James Version (KJV): Published in 1611 by King James I of England, it has a reading level of Grade 12. No other book has had such a tremendous influence on English literature. More poetry than prose, its majestic language, inspired turns of phrase, and poetic rhythms give it great emotional power and make it a classic for memory work even today. However, its archaic sentence structure and word usage can be immensely difficult for new Bible readers.

New International Version (NIV): Published in 1978 by the International Bible Society, it has a reading level of Grade 7.8. The translators sought to make a version that was midway between a literal rendering and a free paraphrase. Their goal was to convey in English the thought of the original writers. Since 1987 it has outsold the KJV, becoming widely accepted for pulpit reading and preaching as well as for personal reading.

New Century Version (NCV): Published in 1987 by Word Publishing, it has a reading level of Grade 3. It was adapted from the International Children's Bible and uses the limited vocabulary of the World Book Encyclopedia. It also uses a simplified sentence structure and familiar place names. A highly readable translation for adults with limited English proficiency, it falters in the expression of figurative or abstract thought.

New Living Translation (NLT): Published in 1996 by Tyndale Press, it has a reading level of Grade 6.3. The Living Bible, which was a paraphrase, underwent a "thorough revision" to produce this translation. The scholars went back to the original languages and sought to produce the closest natural equivalent of the message in natural contemporary English (Dynamic Equivalence).

Good News Translation (GN): Published in 1976 by the American Bible Society, it has a reading level of Grade 6. The method of translation was Dynamic Equivalence, with an emphasis on conveying the meaning of the text in commonly used English. A highly readable translation, it fails to convey the poetic and figurative aspects of the Bible.

Contemporary English Version (CEV): Published in 1995 by the American Bible Society, it has a reading level of Grade 5.6 without sounding "childish." Translators had the mandate to craft a translation that was biblically accurate, reader friendly, and understandable, even for first-time Bible readers.

Living Bible (LB): Published in 1971 by Kenneth Taylor, it has a reading level of Grade 8.3. As a paraphrase it aimed "to say as exactly as possible what the writers of the Scriptures meant, and to say it simply, *expanding* where necessary for a clear understanding by the modern reader."

JB Phillips Translation (JBP): Published in 1958 by JB Phillips, it was one of the first paraphrases. As such, it is highly readable rendering of the New Testament (only) using a fairly sophisticated vocabulary.

The Message (Mes): Published in 1993 by NavPress, it has a reading level of Grade 8.5. It is a free, highly colloquial and interpretative paraphrase whose goal was to "convert the tone, the rhythm, the events, the ideas, into the way we actually think and speak." However, Eugene H. Peterson frequently inserts his particular theological point of view into the text, so while it can be useful as a devotional, it should never be read alone or used as a study Bible. That said, Navigators is a highly respected evangelical organization.

While you will want to own a copy of at least one of these translations of the Bible for your personal reading, there is a wealth of online Bible study resources available today.

➢ **Online resources**

BibleGateway.com http://www.biblegateway.com has the full text of twenty different Bible translations online, including the NIV, NAS, KJV, NLT, CEV, and The Message. Passage Lookup allows you to compare a passage of the Bible in up to five different translations. Simply enter the book of the Bible and chapter number (for example, Matthew 6); verse numbers are optional. Keyword Search returns a list of all the Bible verses in which your keyword(s) appear. You can only search one translation at a time in keyword searches. Study Tools (see Additional Resources) provides fourteen classic Bible commentaries by Reformation leaders and historic evangelists.

Crosswalk.com http://bible.crosswalk.com has the full text of twenty-two different Bible versions online, including the Hebrew and Greek texts and the GN and NCV translations (which are not available anywhere else). The Search field accepts either Bible book and chapter number or keyword(s). The Parallel Bible allows you to compare two different translations. The Online Study Bible provides information from *Strong's Exhaustive Concordance* when you select either KJV or NAS with Strong's Numbers as the translation.

Christian Classics Ethereal Library http://www.ccel.org has an extensive collection of the writings of early church fathers as well as later theologians and preachers. It is maintained by Calvin College. The navigation system is not intuitive, but there is a wealth of information available. In addition, the full text of the JB Phillips Translation is linked to this site at http://www.ccel.org/bible/phillips/JBPhillips.htm. Select a book of the New Testament, and you can scroll though it online.

Endnotes

Lesson #1: The Nature of Love

Adapted from George Feiser's sermon on January 11, 2003, titled Love: the Most Important Thing. In particular: the interpretation of Luke 12:16-21 as What matters most to God; the interpretation of 1 Corinthians 13:1-3 as Without love, nothing I say/know/believe/give/accomplish matters to God; the selfish reasons people give; the phrase, Relationships are far more important than accomplishments; the formulation, Love is a Command, a Choice, a Conduct, and a Commitment; the idea of Tunnels of Chaos and that human love runs out; the suggestions to Learn how mature love responds, Start your day with a reminder to love, Memorize what God says about love, Practice acting in unselfish ways, and Get support from other loving people.

1. During the writing of this lesson, an article by Richard Cohen (a columnist for the *Washington Post*) appeared on the editorial page of my local newspaper. In "Good Men Don't Break Any Eggs," *Dallas Morning News*, Sept. 12, 2003, he eulogized his father, Harry L. Cohen, as a *mensch* (a good man—which is much rarer than a great man) who was faithful in business, family, and friendships, and who died without regrets because he had always given priority to his family over his work.

2. Bruce D. Perry (a consultant in the Columbine school shootings and the Branch Davidian siege) was interviewed by James Ragland for an article that appeared in my local paper, "We Aren't Relating to Our Kids," *Dallas Morning News*, Nov. 7, 2003. It was Dr. Berry's opinion that the poverty of relationships endured by our kids is a bigger threat to them than violence (violence is just easier for us to see).

Lesson #2: Becoming a Giver

Adapted from George Feiser's sermon on January 18, 2003, titled *Kindness: the Act of Love*, which was based on the Parable of the Good Samaritan in Luke

10:30-35. In particular: the priest's attitude of Keep my distance, the Levite's attitude of Curious but uninvolved; the formulation that kindness requires Sensitivity (seeing the needs of people around you), Sympathy (listening to people's pain), and Spontaneity (don't delay, use what you've got); the need to develop Spiritual Radar; the idea that Fear makes us unkind.

Adapted from George Feiser's sermon on March 8, 2003, titled *Respect: the Sign of Love*, which was based on the story in Luke 7:36-48 about a sinful woman who anoints Jesus' feet. In particular: the definition of respect as showing value and honor to others by your actions; the question, Do others feel better or worse after you've left them?; the idea that listening goes beyond words; the importance of keeping your promises; the need to yield your rights and serve others; the formulation that serving is not score-keeping, but showing courtesy and giving your very best to others; the need to get beyond the externals and see the worth in other people.

1.   Kathleen Cotton, "Developing Empathy in Children and Youth," *School Improvement Research Series*, No.13, Northwest Regional Educational Laboratory, 2001, referencing D. Gallo, "Educating for Empathy, Reason and Imagination," *The Journal of Creative Behavior*, Vol. 23, No. 2, 1989, p. 98-115.

2.   Cotton, 2001, referencing S.L. Hahn, "Let's Try a Positive Approach," Foreign Language Annals, Vol. 13, No. 5, 1980, P. 415-417. Students' attitudes toward foreign cultures are more positive if classroom activities begin by stressing its similarities rather than differences.

3.   Cotton, 2001, referencing Gallo, 1989.

Lesson #3: Overcoming Selfishness

Adapted from George Feiser's sermon on January 25, 2003, titled *Envy: the Destroyer of Love*, which was based on the Parable of the Workers in the Vineyard in Matthew 20:1-16. In particular: the five antidotes to envy as Stop comparing yourself to others, Start enjoying God's grace to other people, Be grateful for what you have, Trust God when life seems unfair, and Keep focused on God's plan for you; the idea that we don't always know the whole story behind what we think others have and that we only have grace for our own problems; the understanding that we are not in competition with each other for God's blessings; the concept that Envy is a choice, the warning that God evaluates us on our service.

Adapted from George Feiser's sermon on February 22, 2003, titled *Humility: Love is about Others*. In particular: the idea that pride is always a cover-up for insecurity; defining humility as thinking of others and acting in their best interest; the formulation of practicing humility by Giving preference to others, Being open to suggestions and correction, Admitting when I'm wrong, and Surrendering your plans to God; the insight that a child's humility is rooted in his eagerness to learn; the observation that humble people ask questions, but proud people don't; the concept of Relationally Skimming; the observation that humble people don't defend themselves when criticized.

1. I first heard Dr. Dobson say this on a video teaching tape in the early 1980's. I don't know if the saying was original to him, but to my knowledge he was the one who popularized it. It has now passed into the realm of Christian folk wisdom.

Lesson #4: The Nature of Marriage

I commend *The Case for Marriage: Why Married People Are Happier, Healthier, and Better Off Financially*, written by Linda J. Waite and Maggie Gallagher, New York: Doubleday, 2000, for documenting society's vested interest in successful marriages.

In addition, a comprehensive and heavily footnoted white paper, authored by professors from the Universities of Minnesota, Maryland, Texas, Washington, Denver, Virginia, Chicago and Rutgers, and titled *Why Marriage Matters: Twenty-One Conclusions from the Social Sciences,* is available online at: www.marriagemovement.org/WhyMarriageMatters.html.

I also commend *The Unexpected Legacy of Divorce: A 25 Year Landmark Study*, written by Judith S. Wallerstein, Julia M Lewis and Sandra Blakeslee, New York: Hyperion, 2000, for exploring the long term negative consequences for the children of divorced parents.

1. Hara Marano, "The New Sex Scorecard," *Psychology Today*, Jul/Aug 2003.

2. The Miriam-Webster Online Dictionary defines *synergism* as the "interaction of discrete agencies (as industrial firms), agents (as drugs), or conditions such that the total effect is greater than the sum of the individual effects."

3. Knight Ridder Newspapers, "Experts: Sex Is Good for You," Feb. 13, 2004. Oxytocin promotes emotional bonding, is stimulated by touch, either sexual or mother-child. Endorphins dull perception of pain, relieve stress, provide "runner's high." Serotonins foster feeling of satiety and "afterglow." BBC News, "Expert Explores Chemistry of Love," Feb. 11, 2004. Gareth Leng, University of Edinburgh, believes oxytocin helps forge permanent ties between lovers by "changing the wiring" of billions of cells in the brain. See also Kerstin Uvnas Moberg and Roberta Francis, *The Oxytocin Factor: Tapping the Hormone of Calm, Love, and Healing*, Da Capo Press, 2003.

4. Cal Thomas, "Married With Government," Tribune Media Services, Feb. 21, 2002. James Q. Wilson, "Human Remedies for Social Disorders," *Public Interest*, Spring 1998. William Galston, University of Maryland, is a former domestic policy advisor to Clinton.

5. Thomas, 2002.

6. Wilson, 1998.

7. Phillip Longman, *The Empty Cradle: How Falling Birthrates Threaten World Prosperity*, Basic Books, 2004, as reviewed by William Muehlenberg, Amazon.com. The economic value of children to society is a demographic issue: the need for future workers to support retirees. Longman argues that the financial incentives for parents to raise children have decreased while the cost has increased.

8. Al Sanders, a pioneer with National Religious Broadcasters, presented his research in a short film *Crisis in Morality*, 1961. Direct quotes are available online at: www.ravenhill.org/edwards.htm.

9. John U. Ogbu, *Black American Students in an Affluent Suburb: A Study of Academic Disengagement*, Lea, 2003, as reported by Clarence Page, "Black Parents Must Teach Their Kids to Succeed," *The Chicago Tribune*, Aug. 5, 2003.

10. Abigail Thernstrom and Stephan Thernstrom, *No Excuses: Closing the Racial Gap in Learning*, Simon & Schuster, 2003, as reported by Thomas Sowell, "School Performances," the Creators Syndicate, Sept. 24, 2003.

11. Thernstrom, 2003, as reviewed by Dutch Martin, Amazon.com, Oct. 21,2003.

12. Dennis Rainey, compiled from various articles on www.familylife. com/articles. National study commissioned by FamilyLife in 1995, praying regularly defined as at least 3 times weekly.

13. Marano, 2003.

14. Marano, 2003.

15. The names of Priscilla and Aquila always appear together in the Bible. Twice, Aquila is named first (Acts 18:2 and 1 Corinthians 16:19). Four times, Priscilla is named first (Acts 18:18, Acts 18:26, Romans 16:3, and 2 Timothy 4:19). From this we can infer that Priscilla was a leader just as her husband was. Wherever they lived, the local church met in their home: in Ephesus (1 Corinthians 16:19) and in Rome (Romans 16:5). When Apollos arrived at the (Jewish) synagogue in Ephesus, they invited him home with them and "explained to him the way of God more adequately" (Acts 18:26). That is, he attended the (Christian) church in Ephesus where he heard them teach about Jesus. The plural pronoun indicates that Priscilla was a teacher just as her husband was. Paul called them "my fellow workers in Christ" (Romans 16:3).

16. Proverbs 31:13,19

17. Proverbs 31:24

18. Proverbs 31:18

19. Proverbs 31:16

20. She gets up before dawn to…plan the day's work for her servant girls. Proverbs 31:15 (NLT)

21. The first word for pain is itstsabown (Strong's #6093) which can mean pain, labor, hardship, sorrow, or toil. It only appears 3 times in the Bible, the other two in reference to the toil needed to grow food after the curse (Genesis 3:17 and 5:29). The implication is physical pain.

22. The second word for pain is etseb (Strong's #6089) which can mean pain, hurt, offense, toil, sorrow, labor, or hardship. It appears 7 times in the Bible, and three of those clearly refer to emotional pain (Psalm 127:2, Proverbs 10:22 and 15:1). Even if the nuances of the two words for pain remain somewhat unclear, it is significant that two different words were chosen.

23. The word for children is Ben (Strong's #1121) which can mean son, grandson, child, member of a group, or people of a nation.

24. Sid Kirchheimer, "Mom's Voice is Distinguished in Womb," *WebMD*, May, 14, 2003, and Alison Cook, "Full-Term Fetus Knows Mom's Voice," *Reuters Health*, May 27, 2003, referencing Barbara Kisilevsky and Anthony DeCasper, "Effects of Experience on Fetal Voice Recognition," *Psychological Science*, Vol. 14, Issue 3, May03. Recordings of a poem read by mother and another woman played to full-term unborn babies in China. Babies' heart rates increased for duration of poem recorded by mothers but decreased during poem recorded by others.

25. American Academy of Pediatrics, "Breastfeeding and the Use of Human Milk (RE9729), *Pediatrics*, Vol. 100, No. 6, December 1997, p. 1035-1039.

26. "Formula Additives Boost Small Children's Intelligence in Study," *ScienceDaily*, March 7, 2000. Study was conducted by Retina Foundation of the Southwest in Dallas, funded by the National Institute of Child Health and Human Development, and reported in *Developmental Medicine and Child Neurology*, March 2000.

27. American Academy of Pediatrics, 1997.

28. Roxane Tracey, "Nurturing Linked to Brain Development," *Discovery Channel*, July 19, 2000, referencing an experiment by Michael Meaney at McGill University. Rat pups who received attentive nurturing from their mothers (stroking and grooming) after 3 days performed better on maze tasks and had more developed hippocampuses (brain region responsible for memory and spatial learning).

29. Kancy K. Dess, "Studies Give New Meaning to Hands-On Healing," *Psychology Today*, March, 2000. An interview with Tiffany Field, founder of Touch Research Institutes, about her use of massage therapy on premature infants in NICUs.

30. Sue Iwinski and Gwen Gotsch, "Feeding on Cue," *New Beginnings*, Vol. 20, No. 4, July-August 2003, p. 126. Available online at: www. lalecheleague.org.

31. Martha Farrell Erickson, "The Importance of Attachment in Children's Development," *Early Report*, Vol. 18, No. 2, University of Minnesota, Winter 1991.

32. Kathleen Cotton, "Developing Empathy in Children and Youth," *School Improvement Research Series*, No.13, Northwest Regional Educational Laboratory, 2001, referencing R. Kestenbaum, E.A. Farber and L.A. Sroufe, "Individual Differences in Empathy Among Preschoolers:Relation to Attachment History," *Empathy and Related Emotional Responses*, No. 44, 1989. Children who were most securely attached to their mothers as infants later exhibited the greatest amounts of empathy toward peers. Also referencing Nancy Eisenberg-Berg and P. Mussen, "Empathy and Moral Development in Adolescence," *Developmental Psychology*, Vol 14. No. 2, 1978, p. 185-186. Warm, supportive, non-authoritarian maternal behaviors were positively related with high empathy in boys.

33. Peggy Patten, "Kids Who Care: The Development of Empathy, Care and Compassion," *NPIN Parent News*, January-February 2001, referencing work of Alfie Kohn, *The Brighter Side of Human Nature: Altruism and Empathy in Everyday Life*, Basic Books, 1990. NPIN is National Parenting Information Network, a consortium for early childhood education.

34. Cotton, 2001, referencing D. Gallo, "Educating for Empathy, Reason and Imagination," *The Journal of Creative Behavior*, Vol. 23, No. 2, 1989, p. 98-115. Empathy fosters both creative and critical thinking because it fosters insight into different perspectives. Also referencing A. Kohn, "Caring Kids: The Role of the Schools," *Phi Delta Kappan*, Vol. 72, No. 7, 1991, P. 496-506. Schools with programs to increase empathy in students have higher scores on higher-order reading comprehension.

35. Nancy Low & Associates, Inc., "The Literature Review: A Summary," *Infant Attachment: What We Know Now*, U.S. Dept. of Health and Human Services, June 29, 1991. Also, Terri Smith, "A Look at the Recent Research on Attachment" *Early Report*, Vol. 18, No. 2, University of Minnesota, Winter 1991, referencing D.A. Cohn, "Child-Mother Attachment of Six-Year-Olds

and Social Competence at School," *Child Development*, Vol. 61, 1990, P. 152-162.

36. R. Joseph, "Environmental Influences on Neural Plasticity, the Limbic System, Emotional Development & Attachment," *Child Psychiatry and Human Development*, Vol. 29, 1999, p. 187-203.

37. Joseph, 1999.

38. Low & Associates, 1991.

39. Low & Associates, 1991. Infant attachments to their mothers are Secure (65%), Anxious Avoidant (20%), Anxious Ambivalent (10-15%), or Anxious Disorganized (10-15%). Avoidant attachments are highest among babies who start day care before 6 mos. and spend more than 20 hrs. weekly in non-parental care.

40. NIH News Release, "Only Small Link Found between Hours in Child Care and Mother-Child Interaction," *National Institute of Child Health and Human Development*, Nov. 7, 1999, referencing the NICHHD study. Observers rated taped one-hour play sessions between mother and child for mother's degree of sensitivity, intrusiveness, and respect for child.

41. Joseph, 1999. Joanna Lipari, "Four Things You Need to Know about Raising Baby," *Psychology Today*, July, 2000, referencing the work of Stanley Greenspan, M.D, *Building Healthy Minds: The Six Experiences That Create Intelligence and Emotional Growth In Babies and Young Children*, Perseus Publishing, 1999.

42. Lipari, 2002, quoting Allan N. Schore, assistant clinical professor at UCLA Medical School.

43. Lipari, 2002, quoting Schore on a mother's "emotional synchronization" with her child.

44. Lipari, 2002, quoting Schore.

45. Deborah Hinks, "Analysis of a Child's Needs," *New Generation*, June 1997, referencing the work of Edward C. Melhuish and Peter Moss, *Day Care for Young Children: International Perspectives*, London: Routledge, 1991. Mothers show significantly more affection and responsiveness toward their chil-

dren and are involved in far more communications with them that are paid child care workers.

46. Susan Gilbert, "Two Studies Link Child Care to Behavior Problems," New York Times.com, 2003, referencing Megan R. Gunnar, "Morning to Afternoon Increases in Cortisol Concentrations for Infants and Toddlers at Child Care: Age Differences and Behavioral Correlates," Child Development, Vol. 74, No. 4, July/August, 2003, p. 1006-1020. Also, The Heritage Foundation's Web Memo, FindingID: 5588. Rise in cortisol levels recorded in 35% of infants (aged 3-16 mos.) and 75% of toddlers (aged 16-36 mos.) on days they attended day care.

47. NIH News Release, "Child Care Linked to Assertive, Noncompliant, and Aggressive Behaviors," *National Institute of Child Health and Human Development*, July 16, 2003. Susan Gilbert, "Two Studies Link Child Care to Behavior Problems," *New York Times.com*, 2003, referencing the NICHHD Study of Early Child Care and Youth Development begun in 1991 which is following the development of over 1,300 children. Mothers, child care providers and teachers rated children at age 4½ and again in kindergarten. Increased hours in care correlated with behavior problems regardless of the quality of the child care.

48. NIH News Release, "Only Small Link Found between Hours in Child Care and Mother-Child Interaction," *National Institute of Child Health and Human Development*, Nov. 7, 1999, referencing the NICHHD study. Observers rated taped one-hour play sessions between mother and child for child's mood and degree of engagement with mother. Increased hours in care correlated with child's disengagement from mother.

49. Hinks, 1997, referencing the work of Penelope Leach, *Children First: What Society Must Do—And Is Not Doing—For Children Today*, Vintage, 1995.

50. Claudia Quigg, "Parent-Infant Attachment: The Cradle of Literacy," www.babytalk.org. Parents teach young children simply by including the child in these experiences with language. Also, NIH News Alert, "Children Score Higher on Tests When Child Care Meets Professional Standards," *National Institutes of Health*, July 1, 1999. Children in centers that met the standards scored in the 51st percentile (only average) on school readiness, while children in centers that didn't meet the standards scored in the 39th

percentile (well below average). However, only 10% of infant classrooms and 34% of the 3 year old classrooms met these standards (other ages fell somewhere in-between). This means that children in day care populate the *below* average percentiles for school readiness, implying that the *above* average percentiles are populated by children cared for by their mothers.

Lesson #5: Becoming One

1. For more information, see: www.goodsenseministry.com.

2. Sue Shellenbarger, "Two Incomes, No Sex: Plight of Professionals," *The Wall Street Journal*, April 4, 2003. Richard Reich served as Secretary of Labor in the Clinton administration.

3. Kerry V. Cooke, "Pelvic Floor (Kegel) Exercises for Urinary Incontinence in Women," *Yale New Haven Health*, Oct. 15, 2002. Eva Martin, "Kegel Exercises for Women," *DiscoveryHealth.com*.

4. Focus on the Family web site address is www.family.org. FamilyLife is a division of Campus Crusade for Christ. Its web site address is www.familylife.com.

5. Barry McCarthy, "Sex in the First Two Years of Marriage," First Years and Forever, Vol. 2, Issue 3, November 2002. Barry McCarthy (professor of psychology at American University and a practicing clinical psychologist) writes for the online newsletter of the Family Ministries Office, Archdiocese of Chicago: www.familyministries.org/FirstYearsForever.

Lesson #6: Handling Anger and Conflict

Adapted from George Feiser's sermon on March 15, 2003, titled *Anger: What Emotion Is This?* In particular: the research from the American Demographic Magazine that found 23% openly express their anger in a loud way, 39% bottle it up, and 23% run away from anger; the idea that giving vent to your anger just causes your body to produce more anger; the concept that bitterness is frozen rage; the importance of avoiding people who stir up your anger; the link between worry and anger and the antidote of prayer; the susceptibility to anger when you're physically or emotionally tired; the anger that results when reality doesn't match our expectations; the need to dwell on the good in your life.

1. Bernice Kanner, "Turning the Other Cheek," *American Demographics*, Feb98, Vol. 20, Issue 2, p. 39.

2. Holly Parker, "Nonviolent Venting," *Psychology Today*, July/Aug 99. Experiments by Brad Bushman, Iowa State University, found that participants who hit a punching bag before responding to an insulting situation expressed twice as much anger as the control group.

3. Edward C. Suarez, James G. Lewis, and Cynthia Kuhn, *Brain, Behavior and Immunity*, Vol. 16, No. 6, as reported in "Hostility Associated with Immune Function," *Monitor on Psychology*, Vol. 34, No. 3, March 2003: highly hostile men have higher levels of TNF, an immune system protein linked to cardiovascular disease. *Circulation*, Volume 101, No. 17, as reported in "Angry Thoughts, At-Risk Hearts," *Monitor on Psychology*, Vol. 34, No. 3, March 2003: people most prone to anger were almost three times more likely to have a heart attack than those with low anger. Karina Davidson, *International Journal of Behavioral Medicine*, Vol. 6, No. 3, 1998, as reported in the same article: people who scored high on a measure of constructive anger returned to their baseline blood pressure levels quickly (often within 5 minutes) while those with low constructive anger scores took up to 90 minutes to reduce their blood pressure after an irritating incident.

4. Timothy W. Smith and Linda C. Gallo, Psychosomatic Medicine, Vol. 61, No. 4, 1999, as reported in "Angry Thoughts, At-Risk Hearts," *Monitor on Psychology*, Vol. 34, No. 3, March 2003: husbands with high scores for hostile and suspicious attitudes (and their wives!) had larger increases in blood pressure than those with low scores during discussions of stressful marital issues; interacting with hostile husbands increased the stressfulness of the discussion for their wives.

5. Diane Sollee, "What's the Number One Predictor of Divorce?" Smart Marriages: The Coalition for Marriage, Family and Couples Education, L.L.C., available online at: www.smartmarriages.com.

6. Peggy Patten, "Marital Relationships, Children, and Their Friends: What's the Connection? An Interview with E. Mark Cummings," *NPIN Parent News*, May-June 2000. Refer to: E. Mark Cummings and Patrick T. Davies,

Children and Marital Conflict: The Impact of Family Dispute and Resolution, New York: The Guilford Press, 1994. Cummings is chair of the Department of Psychology at Notre Dame University.

7. Patten, 2000.

8. Patten, 2000.

9. The Miriam-Webster Online Dictionary defines *synthesis* as "the combining of often diverse conceptions into a coherent whole," or "the dialectic combination of thesis and antithesis into a higher stage of truth."

Lesson #7: Healing Hurts through Forgiveness

Adapted from George Feiser's sermon on March 22, 2003, titled *Love Is About the F-word: Forgiveness*. In particular: the difference between being wounded and being wronged; the idea that only the victim can forgive; the formulation that forgiveness is not Conditional upon someone else's response or Minimizing the hurt or Forgetting what happened or Resuming a relationship; the need for the offender to demonstrate repentance, make restitution, and rebuild trust in order to resume the relationship; the need to relinquish your right to get even; the realization that resentment makes you miserable; the need to forgive so that you can be filled with God's love and move on with your life; the idea that forgiveness is often a process; the technique of the Open Chair and the Unmailed Letter; the importance in remembering how much Jesus has forgiven you.

Steve Lucas suggested concluding the course with a Oneness Covenant. The term originated with Dennis Rainey, Executive Director of FamilyLife, online at: www.familylife.com. However, we preferred to have each couple write their own covenant instead of simply affirming the FamilyLife covenant. We wanted couples to think about the nature of the commitment they were making to one another and to define their points of unity.

1. The Miriam-Webster Online Dictionary defines *restitution* as "an act of restoring to a previous state" or "a condition of being restored, as in, giving an equivalent for some injury." We cannot restore ourselves because we cannot change ourselves. Nor do we have anything to offer God to pay for our sins.

2. Franz Schurmann, "The Bells Toll—For Serbs: History Repeats Itself," Pacific News Service, March 24, 1999, available online as Jinn Magazine: www.pacificnews.org/jinn.

3. John Derbyshire, "Our Lost Land," *National Review Online*, Oct. 18, 2001, available at: www.nationalreview.com. Historical context of the quote from Osama bin Laden on October 7, 2001, which concludes, "We cannot accept that Palestine will become Jewish."

4. James Carroll, "The Bush Crusade," *The Nation*, Sept. 20, 2004, focuses on the Crusades' atrocities against Jews, Muslims, and Orthodox Christians. In contrast, Austin Miles, "President Bush and the 'C' Word," *BushCountry.org*, May 13, 2004, focuses on the Muslim atrocities that provoked the Crusades.

5. Al Lupnitz taught us about the healing of memories at Longview Christian Fellowship, in Longview, Texas. The curriculum was developed by S. Don Ballenger, *Word Based Counseling: Basic 1*, 1983.

Lesson #8: Speaking the Truth with Love

Adapted from George Feiser's sermon on March 29, 2003, titled *Tough Love*. In particular: using excepts from 1 & 2 Corinthians to analyze how Paul shared tough things with the church; the idea that closeness and confrontation go hand in hand in relationships; the need to check your motives in speaking; the importance of introductions; the need for recent examples; the equation Truth + Tact + Timing = Transformation; the idea that you cannot be persuasive if you are abrasive; the importance of giving words of affirmation; the use of the conjunction "and" instead of "but" in linking affirmation with correction; the courage it takes to be willing to risk rejection by the person.

Lesson #9: The Nature of Commitment

1. "The Solemnization of Matrimony," *Anglican Book of Common Prayer*, 1662. Husband's vow is quoted; wife's vow promises "to love, honor, and to obey" but is otherwise identical.

2. Steve Lucas and his wife, Angela, introduced us to the concept of the Family Staff Meeting at a marriage retreat for our church. Dr. David Ferguson and

his wife, Teresa, developed this idea as part of their *Intimate Encounters* workshops, see online: www.greatcommandment.net. The Fergusons provide a structured format for the Family Staff Meeting, but I have suggested that couples adapt the idea freely according to their needs and their personalities.

Pastoral Counseling Session

The need for this lesson became apparent in a conversation with Stan and Marti Martin at Grace Community Church. We decided that the appropriate venue for a couple to discuss sexual abstinence, particularly when they were already living together, was in a pastoral setting. The lesson is provided to facilitate that discussion.

I commend the articles by Glenn T. Stanton, the Director of Social Research and Cultural Affairs for Focus on the Family. His articles are available online at: www.family.org/cforum.

1.   James Q. Wilson, *The Marriage Problem: How Our Culture Has Weakened Families*, Harper Collins, 2002, p. 3, puts the rate at 56%. Popenoe and Whitehead, 2002, p. 3, put the rate at 50%.

2.   Lee Robins and Darrel Regier, Psychiatric Disorders in America: The Epidemiologic Catchment Area Study, New York: The Free Press, 1991, p. 64.

3.   Larry L. Bumpass, James A. Sweet, and Andrew Cherlin, "The Role of Cohabitation in Declining Rates of Marriage," *Journal of Marriage and the Family* 53, 1991, P. 913-927.

4.   Linda J. Waite and Maggie Gallagher, The Case for Marriage: Why Married People are Happier, Healthier, and Better Off Financially, New York: Doubleday, 2000, p. 93.

5.   Waite and Gallagher, p. 93.

6.   Kersti Yllo and Murray A. Straus, "Interpersonal Violence among Married and Cohabiting Couples," *Family Relations* 30, 1981, p. 339-347.

7.   Yllo and Straus, p. 339-347.

8. Todd K. Shackelford, "Cohabitation, Marriage and Murder," *Aggressive Behavior* 27, 2001, p. 284-291.

9. David Popenoe and Barbara Dafoe Whitehead, "Should We Live Together? What Young Adults Need to Know about Cohabitation Before Marriage," *The National Marriage Project*, Rutgers University, 2002, p. 9.

10. Alan Booth and David Johnson, "Premarital Cohabitation and Marital Success," Journal *of Family Issues* 9, 1988, p. 255-272.

11. Catherine Cohan and Stacey Kleinbaum, "Toward a Greater Understanding of the Cohabitation Effect: Premarital Cohabitation and Marital Communication," *Journal of Marriage and Family* 64, 2002, p. 180-192.

12. Michael D. Newcomb and P.M. Bentler, "Assessment of Personality and Demographic Aspects of Cohabitation and Marital Success," Journal of Personality Assessment 44, 1980, p.11-24.

13. Newcomb and Bentler, p.11-24.

14. Linda J. Waite, Frances Goldschieder and C. Witsberger, "Nonfamily Living and the Erosion of Traditional Family Orientations Among Adults," *American Sociological Review* 51, 1986, p. 541-554.

15. Neil Bennett, Ann Blanc and David Bloom, "Commitment and Modern Union: Assessing the Link Between Premarital Cohabitation and Subsequent Marital Stability," *American Sociological Review* 53, 1988, p. 127-138.

16. Neil Clark Warren, "The Cohabitation Epidemic," *Focus on the Family Magazine*, 2003.

About the Use of Scripture

More information about the various Bible translations can be found at the International Bible Society web site (www.ibs.org/bibles/translations), the Zondervan Publishing web site (www.zondervanbibles.com/translations.htm), and at a quirky but reliable personal web site (www.kenanderson.net/bible, select Versions).

0-595-33867-4

Printed in the United States
88673LV00004B/220-231/A